The BIG Book of
Sales Games

Other Books in <u>The Big Book of Business Games</u> Series Include:

The Big Book of Business Games
The Big Book of Team Building Games
The Big Book of Presentation Games
The Big Book of Customer Service Training Games
The Big Book of Stress Management Training Games (forthcoming)

The BIG Book of
Sales Games

Quick, Fun Activities for Improving Selling Skills or Livening Up a Sales Meeting

Peggy Carlaw

Vasudha Kathleen Deming

McGraw-Hill

New York   San Francisco   Washington, D.C.   Auckland   Bogotá
Caracas   Lisbon   London   Madrid   Mexico City   Milan
Montreal   New Delhi   San Juan   Singapore
Sydney   Tokyo   Toronto

McGraw-Hill

A Division of The McGraw-Hill Companies

2 3 4 5 6 7 8 9 0 DOC DOC 9 0 3 2 1 0 9

ISBN 0-07-134336-9

The sponsoring editor for this book was Richard Narramore, the editing supervisor was John Morriss, the designer was Peggy Carlaw, and the production supervisor was Suzanne W. B. Rapcavage. It was set by Impact Learning Systems in Stone Sans and Gill Sans.

Printed and bound by R. R. Donnelley & Sons Company.

McGraw-Hill books are available at special quantity discounts to use as premiums and sales promotions, or for use in corporate training programs. For more information, please write to the Director of Special Sales, McGraw-Hill, 11 West 19th Street, New York, NY 10011. Or contact your local bookstore.

Contents

Introduction

To be a successful salesperson, one must be adept at a battery of skills: listening, questioning, presenting, overcoming objections, building rapport, etc. It also doesn't hurt to have flawless intuition, dauntless optimism, and thicker than usual skin.

But as we see it, the most important "skill" a good salesperson exhibits is a true willingness to serve customers—to fit their needs; to solve their problems; to inform, enlighten, or unburden them.

With this book, we've endeavored to give you a way of helping your salespeople to embrace this ethic of service and to consistently put it to work.

The games in this book are fun, motivational activities centered around skill learning and skill use. They build confidence, lift morale, spark enthusiasm, stimulate creativity and ultimately achieve results in the real-time sales environment. We've consistently found that salespeople look forward to these games and become fully immersed while playing. You may be surprised at which members of your sales team come to life when game time arrives!

The games are designed to be administered by anyone who manages, supervises, or trains salespeople. Many of them can be adapted for use by individual salespeople (refer to the following section, "If You're on Your Own." They're meant to be played by anyone, in any industry, who holds a sales position: account executives, field reps, telemarketers, retail sales staff, etc.

Some of the games are quick, fun energizers that serve to raise participants' awareness of sales issues. Others are full-scale activities that teach a skill and offer participants the opportunity to practice the skill in an informal, non-threatening environment. There are any number of ways you can use the games: as stand-alone training activities, as warm-ups to a more intensive training session, or in combination with one another to constitute a comprehensive sales training event.

Alternatively, you can use these ten- to thirty-minute games at your staff meetings, Friday afternoon discussion groups, brown-bag lunches, and anywhere else you see fit. You don't even have to tell participants it's "training"!

The games will not only motivate your salespeople to do their job better, but will also inspire them to offer a level of service that brings new meaning and motivation to their job. In turn, their success will help your organization to prosper—both in its quality of life and in its quantity of sales.

How to Use This Book

The book contains 50 games—long and short, simple and complex—that address twelve different categories of sales. We've endeavored to make the games straightforward and easy to deliver. Following is our advice to you for getting the most out of this book and out of your sales employees.

Tips for Success:

- Prepare for your training session by taking the time to thoroughly review each game beforehand. The better you understand the objective, flow, and tone of each game, the more successful the training will be.

- Keep in mind that these are games. If you maintain a playful, enthusiastic approach, you'll find that the participants too will feel comfortable and motivated to partake.

- Whenever possible, bring in some real-time examples of problems and situations you've observed at your organization. This will help participants to transfer the learning to their on-the-job environment.

- Play the role of facilitator rather than teacher. The most effective learning comes when you guide the participants and they make the discovery.

- Adapt the games to the climate and culture in which your employees work. If they respond well to rewards, then offer candy, gift certificates, or other small rewards at the conclusion of each game. If your salespeople can be trusted to have fun-spirited competitions (as opposed to heated battles), then go ahead and turn the games into competitions. Each group can choose a team name and can show their team spirit by clapping, cheering, etc.

- Except for a few props, we've given you everything you need to successfully facilitate the games. Nevertheless, we encourage you to be creative in expanding upon the games in any way that will make them meaningful for the participants.

- All the games lend themselves to further discussion and review. Follow up on what participants learned by debriefing the game, creating job aids, or establishing a game plan for ongoing practice and review.

If You're on Your Own

Soon after we began developing this book, it occurred to us that many of the games could be effective without a group setting. Though it seemed somewhat odd to think that a salesperson might play a "game" by himself, we realized that many of the games are simply skill-improvement exercises set in a game format. And so, by extension it seems that this book can also be used as a workbook for self-motivated salespeople in any field.

We've indicated below the games that we feel provide valuable learning even if you're "playing" on your own. At the end of each of these activities, you'll find the heading "If You're on Your Own." The information under this heading guides you in adapting the game for individual use.

The following games can be done if you're on your own:

It Begins Within

Activities for Motivating Yourself or Your Team

The Greatest Sales Stories Ever Told

In a Nutshell

In this upbeat activity, salespeople tell their favorite sales stories and identify what they did well and what effect these efforts had on the customer. The activity is suitable for new hires as well as seasoned veterans and is especially useful when salespeople need some motivation.

Time

10–15 minutes.

What You'll Need

A certificate or fun "award" for each salesperson.

What to Do

Ask salespeople to think about their biggest sales achievement to date. It may be their largest sale or even a small sale that was particularly challenging.

After a short time, ask salespeople to take another few minutes to identify what, specifically, they did that made this their biggest sales achievement and what effect these efforts had on the customer.

Ask each participant to stand and tell the group about the salesperson's biggest achievement. Present each salesperson with an "award" recognizing his or her achievement.

Personal Selling Power

In a Nutshell

In this activity, salespeople review skills that are essential to the sales role, assess their own competence in each skill, and develop an action plan for improving their proficiency. This activity helps new employees understand the assets possessed by top-notch sales representatives and gives all salespeople an opportunity to review their assets and their opportunities for improvement.

Time

10–15 minutes.

What You'll Need

One copy of the handouts on pages 7 through 9 for each participant.

What to Do

Distribute the handouts on pages 7 and 8. Give participants five to ten minutes to complete the activity.

Then distribute the handout on page 9 and ask each participant to develop an action plan to improve two skills.

If You Have More Time

Make another copy of the Action Plan Worksheet on page 9. Put participants into pairs. Each participant will write the skills he or she wants to improve on the Action Plan Worksheet on the line titled "Your skill." The participants will then trade worksheets with their partners.

Each participant will create an action plan to help his or her partner become a Super Star in the areas listed on the worksheet. Allow five minutes for this activity.

After five minutes, have participants trade action plans and give them several minutes to review the plans.

Ask participants to review their action plans from time to time in order to improve their proficiency in each skill.

If You're on Your Own

Review the handout on page 7 and complete page 8. Develop an action plan to improve two skills by completing page 9. Review your action plans on a daily or weekly basis.

Personal Selling Power Assets

Whether you plan a lifelong career in sales or view your present job as a stepping stone to something else, the skills you use to serve your customers and make a sale will be assets in any field you choose. What's more, a good attitude is key to success anywhere, anytime. Salespeople who stand out in their work are:

- Friendly
- Quick
- Efficient
- Eager to please
- Knowledgeable
- Optimistic
- Diligent
- Able to understand customers' requests

- Attentive
- Creatively helpful
- Empathetic
- Poised
- Upbeat
- Honest and fair
- Solution-oriented

These sales representatives always:

- Listen attentively.
- Maintain a positive attitude.
- Act with integrity.
- Thoroughly understand their product's features and benefits.
- Avoid technical terms or fancy words.
- Give customers a feeling of confidence in them, the information they give, and the company.
- Make every customer feel important.
- Meet customer needs.
- Ask for the sale.

Assets and Opportunities

Although you may naturally be stronger in some areas than in others, your job provides you with the opportunity to master each and every one of the Personal Selling Power Assets.

Read through the list of assets again and put each item onto the chart below according to your own proficiency. Be honest. No one is watching.

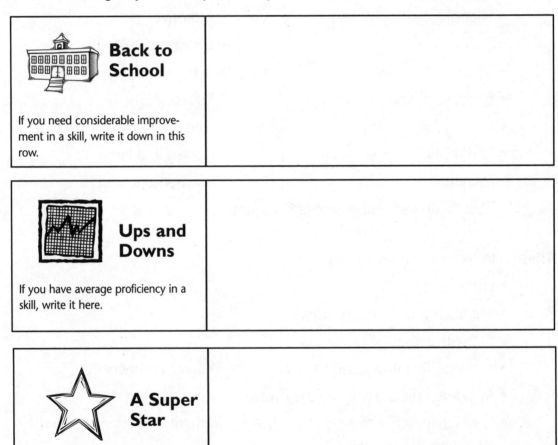

Back to School

If you need considerable improvement in a skill, write it down in this row.

Ups and Downs

If you have average proficiency in a skill, write it here.

A Super Star

Write your best skills, the assets you bring to your job, in this row.

Action Plan Worksheet

Your skill: _____

Your action plan: _____

_____

_____

_____

_____

_____

_____

Your skill: _____

Your action plan: _____

_____

_____

_____

_____

_____

_____

Mission Possible

In a Nutshell

In this activity, participants create a mission statement for themselves or their sales team. This activity is ideal for injecting a high level of enthusiasm and bringing a new sense of meaning to work.

Time

20–25 minutes.

What You'll Need

Copies of your corporate mission statement, if you have one, or copies of other companies' mission statements that you find inspiring. Blank flip-chart paper and marker pens (for each three to five salespeople).

What to Do

Discuss the concept of a mission statement. Hand out your corporate mission statement (or those from other companies if you don't have one).

Put salespeople into groups of three to five and give each group a piece of flip-chart paper and a marker pen. Explain that their job will be to work together to come up with a brief mission statement for their department.

Review the overhead on page 14 and tell the sales-people to discuss the answers to their questions before beginning to write their mission statement.

Allow ten minutes for this part of the activity. If there is more than one group, ask each group to select a spokesperson to present its mission statement to the class.

Listen to the mission statements and discuss as needed. Be sure the mission statements do not contradict your company mission statement.

If there is more than one group, ask each group to appoint one member to represent the group on a commit-tee to finalize the mission statement. Suggest that the committee meet at lunch or arrange for committee mem-bers to have time off during work to finalize the statement over the course of the next week. When the mission state-ment is complete, obtain the finalized mission statement and print an attractive copy to be posted in the depart-ment's work area. Also consider printing smaller copies for each salesperson to post in his or her work area. If possi-ble, bring the
salespeople together again to present the final mission statement.

If You Have More Time

Have each salesperson write a personal mission statement that complements the statement written by the depart-ment. Give them nice paper so that they can print the statements and post them at their desks.

If You're on Your Own

Review your company's mission statement or those of other companies. Read through the questions on page 14, applying them to yourself rather than your sales team. Take some time to develop your own sales mission statement, and print the final version on nice paper. Keep it in your work area or your appointment book so you can refer to it often.

Defining Your Mission

- Why do customers remember us?

- How do customers feel after they deal with us?

- What do customers tell their friends about us?

- In what ways do we help one another in our department?

- How does our department support the general aim of our company?

Write Yourself a Letter

In a Nutshell

Salespeople write themselves a letter from a fictional customer. Each letter highlights three aspects of the salesperson's behavior or attitude that made a positive impression on the customer. The letter also points out what effect each action had on the customer. This activity is meant to focus salespeople's attention on the things they do well, and to motivate them to continue with these efforts.

Time

10–15 minutes.

What You'll Need

One copy of the handouts on page 17 and 18 for each salesperson. Salespeople will need paper and pens.

What to Do

Distribute the handouts. Read out the sample letter on page 17, and tell salespeople they'll be writing a similar letter to themselves. Ask them to pay close attention to what the customer says about the impact of the salesperson's actions and attitude. If you're conducting this as a group activity, copy the sample letter onto an overhead transparency and display it during the letter-writing activity.

Tell salespeople to think about their own interactions with customers, and about how their attitude and behavior affects customers in a positive way. They should complete the form letter on page 18 as if they were a customer. If necessary, they can change the printed words slightly.

Allow about 10–15 minutes for this activity.

If You're on Your Own

Read the letter on page 17 and then complete the form letter on page 18 as if you were a customer.

Dear Terry:

I'm writing to thank you personally for the service you provided when my husband Ray and I were selecting kitchen equipment for our new restaurant.

You helped us in a number of ways. First, you respected our budget. This allowed us to find quality equipment within our price range. I also appreciated the way you pointed out helpful information regarding use of space in the kitchen. Your expertise made me feel like a valued customer.

Finally, I wanted to say thanks for your personal touch and supportive attitude. It convinced me that you sincerely want us to succeed in this very competitive industry.

Thank you again. And keep up the good work!

Sincerely,

Elma

Elma Homestead
Ma's Diner

Dear _____:

I wanted to write to thank you personally for the service you provided _____

_____
(when)
_____

You helped me out in a number of ways. First, you _____
(action)
_____ This _____
(effect)
_____

_____

I also appreciated the way you _____
(action)

_____

Your _____
(sales strength or skill)
made me feel like a valued customer.

Finally, I wanted to say thanks for_____
(action)
I think it will really make a difference to _____
(effect)

Keep up the good work!

Sincerely,

_____
(customer's name)

Salesperson of the Year

In a Nutshell

Salespeople "plan" the awards ceremony held in their honor as a result of being named Salesperson of the Year. This activity provides an opportunity for the salespeople to visualize a successful result of their work, and it gives the manager or trainer insight into the character and motivations of each salesperson. Note: One variation of this activity is to have salespeople write a brief article (for a fictional newsletter or newspaper) describing the celebration held in their honor.

Time

10–15 minutes.

What You'll Need

Salespeople will need paper and pen.

What to Do

Tell salespeople to imagine they've just been named Salesperson of the Year. Their task is to plan the awards ceremony to be held in their honor. There's no budget, and the only guideline is that they can't break any company rules. Allow about ten minutes for them to write.

Encourage salespeople to think creatively and to have some fun with this. It's their opportunity to plan their "dream celebration"! To get them started, ask them to consider the following:

- Theme
- Number of people in attendance
- Venue
- Time of day
- Activities
- Menu

When salespeople have finished, go around the room and ask each person to share their plans.

If You're on Your Own

Write an article for your local newspaper or company newsletter describing the ceremony held in your honor as Salesperson of the Year. For inspiration, review the article every time you review your sales goals.

2

What Do You Know?

Games to Enhance Product Knowledge

Product Knowledge Quiz

EP-4663	R-334J	$$$$
10 points	10 points	10 points
20 points	20 points	20 points
30 points	30 points	30 points
40 points	40 points	40 points

In a Nutshell

In this rousing game, salespeople play a game similar to *Jeopardy!* to test their product knowledge. This game is suitable for new hires or for seasoned salespeople.

Time

15 minutes.

What You'll Need

A flip-chart and markers. (Optional: A package of 5" x 7" index cards.) A small prize for the winning team.

What to Do

Select five product categories and develop four questions and answers for each. Within each category, the questions should progress from simple to difficult.

Prepare a *Jeopardy!* game board using flip-chart paper. List the product categories across the top and assign a point total to each row of question (e.g., 10 points for row one, 20 points for row two, etc). If you prefer, you can use 5"x 7" index cards with an "answer" written on the back of each card.

Form teams of two to four salespeople. Advise salespeople that to start the game, you will give an answer from the top left of the game board. They must respond with the corresponding question. When everyone on the team agrees with the question, everyone should raise a hand.

Call on the first team that has all hands raised. You may call on any salesperson on the team to give a question to the answer you read. If the question is correct, the team gets the points; if the question is incorrect, the team loses the points. The team that develops the correct question gets to select the next answer.

Keep track of which answers have been given by crossing the answer off the game board or removing the index card. Keep track of any questions salespeople have difficulty answering. You can come back to those questions for review when the game is over.

Keep score as you play the game, and reward the winning team with a small prize.

So What?

In a Nutshell

This game taps the group's collective brain power by having each person come up with benefits that correspond to various features of the sales group's products. It's a fun learning game that drives home the difference between features and benefits and enhances salespeople's product knowledge.

Time

Approximately 10–20 minutes, depending on the number and complexity of products.

What You'll Need

Several index cards. Depending on the knowledge level of the salespeople, you may want to make an overhead transparency (or copies to hand out) of page 170.

What to Do

There are two variations of this game. The first one requires you to prepare index cards ahead of time by writing one feature of one product at the top of each card. If you opt for the second variation, distribute blank index cards to the salespeople and ask each person to select one feature of one product and write it at the top of the card (make sure there are no duplications before moving on to the next step).

Arrange the seated salespeople in a circle and tell them to pass their index card to the person on their right. Each person should now write a benefit that corresponds to the product feature they have in front of them. Allow 30–60 seconds for each pass (the game gets progressively harder because the more obvious benefits will be chosen first). Continue until all salespeople have written on all cards.

End the game by having each salesperson read out what's on his or her original index card.

Think on Your Feet!

In a Nutshell

This is an active, high-spirited game in which salespeople hear a product feature and must immediately respond with a corresponding benefit. Variations of this game can be played with salespeople at all levels.

Time

Usually 3–5 minutes.

What You'll Need

A small, soft ball or similar object. Prepare a list of several product features before beginning the game.

Depending on the knowledge level of the salespeople, you may want to make an overhead transparency (or copies to hand out) of page 170.

What to Do

Ask salespeople to stand in a circle, a few feet apart. Tell them you'll toss the ball to someone as you call out the feature of one of their products. The person to whom the ball is tossed must catch the ball and respond with a corresponding benefit. They then toss the ball to someone else, who must respond with another benefit. After every three or four tosses, you should call out another product feature.

Continue the game until everyone has had at least one turn.

3

Before You Say Hello

Activities for Sales Call Preparation

Who, What, Where, When, Why?

In a Nutshell

In this fast-paced game salespeople answer the five "Ws" to help them prepare for a sales call. The activity is suited for all levels of salespeople.

Time

5–10 minutes.

What You'll Need

A stopwatch, Post-it note pads of various colors, and a flip-chart or white board with a space for each team to post its self-stick notes. Divide the space into five columns, and assign each column of the following headings: Who, What, Where, When, Why.

What to Do

Prepare a fictional company profile that represents a company with business potential for your salespeople. It might include some of the following information:

- Company name and address
- Information about the company—its locations, size, products or services sold, etc.
- Names and profiles of various decision makers or influencers throughout the company

- Information about the company's relationship with your company (a loyal customer, doing business with the competition, etc.).
- Brief history of prior meetings, if any, with the decision makers or influencers mentioned earlier.

Review the importance of pre-call planning with salespeople, then divide them into small groups. (Each group should have a different color of Post-it note pads.)

Describe the prospective company and explain that you will read a question for each of the five Ws—who, what, where, when, and why. Each group will have thirty seconds to discuss the question, write an answer on the self-stick note, and post it on the flip-chart or white board. No running!

The first team with an answer on the board gets one point. The questions you will read are:

- **W**hom do you want to call on in the company?
- **W**hat outcome do you want?
- **W**here would be the best place to meet?
- **W**hen would be the best time to meet?
- **W**hy do you want to meet them?

When you've finished the game, give a small reward to the team with the most points, then ask the teams to collect all their Post-it notes, take one to two minutes to look at their overall call strategy, then present it to the group.

Close by pointing out that while the game was quick and fun, pre-call planning is an essential part of account strategy.

If You're on Your Own

Ask yourself the five questions above before you set each sales call appointment. Be sure to plan an overall account strategy so that you use your time wisely and achieve optimal results.

WIIFM (What's in It for Me?)

In a Nutshell

Salespeople practice focusing on customer benefits by answering the question "What's in it for me?" This game is suitable for salespeople of all levels who have basic product knowledge, but it is best when played with salespeople at similar levels of experience who are comfortable speaking in front of a group.

Time

15–30 minutes.

What You'll Need

Poker chips or other "WIIFM" tokens.

What to Do

Review the concept of features and benefits and point out that the most successful salespeople are those who focus on ways that their products or services will benefit buyers.

Give each salesperson two WIIFM tokens. Explain that salespeople will come up to the front of the room one at a time and make a short presentation to the group about a product with which they are familiar. Assign a presentation length based on the number of salespeople presenting and the time available for the game. If you have a large number of salespeople and a short amount of time, divide the participants into two or three groups.

While one salesperson is presenting, other salespeople will be listening for benefits. If the salesperson presenting gives a feature of the product or service without its corresponding benefit, someone from the audience can stand up and ask "WIIFM?" at which point the salesperson should respond with a benefit and then continue his or her presentation. (WIIFM tokens are given out to be sure that some people don't monopolize the game.)

Present a small prize, certificate, or award to those salespeople who did not collect any WIIFM tokens.

If You're on Your Own

Tape record one of your typical sales presentations. Play the tape back and see if you presented any features without the corresponding benefits.

Super Sleuthing

In a Nutshell

Pairs compete in a mock contest to come up with background information they need about a company before making a sales call and with potential sources for finding that information.

Time

15–20 minutes.

What You'll Need

A fictitious profile of a company that is a prospective buyer of your product or service. A "Super Sleuth Award" to present to the winning team.

What to Do

Tell salespeople they'll be working in pairs and participating in a Super Sleuth contest to determine the team with the most creative ideas for uncovering information about a prospective buyer.

The purpose of the contest is to come up with the three most critical things they need to know about a prospective company before making a sales call and with creative ways of finding that information. Encourage salespeople to be as creative as possible in coming up with their ideas. (You can discuss ethics later!)

Assign pairs and read or hand out the fictitious company profile. Give participants about ten minutes to come up with their ideas, and then go around the room and have each pair announce the information they want to acquire and their ideas about how to acquire it.

Take a vote to see which team wins the contest and present that team with the Super Sleuth Award.

Hitting the Mark

In a Nutshell

Salespeople learn the importance of setting concrete call objectives before making a sales presentation—either on the phone or in person—by competing in teams to identify well-defined call objectives. It is suitable for all levels of salespeople.

Time

10–15 minutes.

What You'll Need

Overhead transparencies or flip-charts containing the information on pages 43 and 44.

What to Do

Review the overheads. Use the following example: The purpose of an initial phone call might be to qualify someone for business potential. The measurement might be to complete a qualifying interview with a decision maker. Remind salespeople that the objective of each contact should be to move the sale forward.

Divide salespeople into small teams. Tell them that you'll read a call objective. Their goal is to decide whether it is a valid call objective or not. Once they've decided they should all raise their hands. Call on the first team with all hands raised. You can ask any member of the team to give the answer and the reason why the team selected that answer. Give each team one point for each correct answer. Offer the team with the most points a small prize or other type of acknowledgment.

Keep the game moving quickly. When you've finished the game, review each poorly constructed call objective and ask salespeople to develop a better one.

Call Objectives

1. You're making a call to follow up on a lead from a trade show. Your call objective is to remind the customer about your new line of desk accessories.

    Not good. It focused on the salesperson, not on what the customer will commit to to move the sale to the next step.

2. You're making a final presentation after months of client meetings. Your call objective is to get the client to sign a purchase order which will make you their sole source supplier.

    Good. It's measurable and focuses on the client's action.

3. You're meeting with the purchasing committee and your call objective is to make a presentation about your company and the two product lines that will meet the needs identified during earlier meetings.

   Not good. It focused on the salesperson's activity, not what action the customer will take to move the sale forward.

4. You've had Acme Paperweights as a customer for many years. As a matter of fact, they're your top customer for your premium resin. You're going to call the manufacturing manager and your call objective is to have the manufacturing manager introduce you to the new purchasing manager.

   Good. It indicates the steps the manufacturing manager will take to help you begin to build a relationship with the new purchasing manager.

5. You're following up on a referral from your networking club. Your call objective is to introduce yourself and get the referral to agree to a date and time for an appointment.

   Good. It's measurable and focuses on the referral's action.

6. You work for a weight-loss center and you're meeting with a client who has just reached his goal weight. Your call objective is to point out the benefits of signing up for a lifetime membership.

   Not good. It doesn't include what the customer will agree to.

7. Your company is hosting a free seminar on technology in the next decade. Your objective is to let the prospect know the date, time, and place.

   Not good. It focused on the salesperson's activity, not on what the prospect will do.

If You're on Your Own

Use the information on pages 43 and 44 to help you develop call objectives for each sales call this week.

Call Objective: What you want the buyer to do by the end of your call in order to move a step closer to gaining a sale or continuing a relationship with a customer.

A call objective has two aspects:

- Purpose   The reason for making the call

- Measurement   Actions taken during or following the call that indicate your level of success

Call objectives are:

- Results-oriented, <u>not</u> activity-oriented

- Focused on what the buyer will do, <u>not</u> on what you will do.

Examples:

- To set up a meeting with the Vice President of Purchasing

- To get the buyer to agree to a three-month trial package

You Look Marvelous!

In a Nutshell

In this game, salespeople review various pictures to determine the importance of body language and appearance in adding meaning to communication. The objective is for participants to learn basic techniques they can use to be sure their body language and appearance are sending the message they intend. This game is ideal for introducing the concept of visual communication.

Time

10–15 minutes.

What You'll Need

One copy of the handout on page 48 for each participant. A blank flip-chart or white board and marker.

What to Do

Distribute one copy of the handout to each participant. Ask participants to work in small groups to determine what they think each person does for a living and what each person is feeling. They should also discuss why they came to these conclusions.

After five to seven minutes, ask each group to report their findings. List any points they made regarding body language and attire on the flip-chart or white board.

Discussion Questions

Q: How do your body language and attire affect your communication with your prospect or customer?

A: *A customer can tell you're friendly, confident, and interested if you dress appropriate to your position, if you maintain an open stance, and if you lean back slightly to show you're relaxed or lean forward slightly to indicate you're interested (Figures 4 and 5). A customer may perceive you as defensive if you close up and cross your arms (Figure 1). A customer may show you that he or she is angry or upset by maintaining a frontal, rigid stance (Figures 2 and 3).*

Q: What kind of posture can you exhibit to help defuse a challenging situation, such as when a prospect or customer is complaining?

A: *Keep an open posture to show that you aren't defensive and lean forward slightly to show that you are interested in helping the customer find a solution.*

Q: What, if anything, would you like to change about your body language or attire to help you present a better image of yourself and your product or service?

A: *Field answers.*

If You're on Your Own

Take a look at the figures on page 48 and think about what each person does for a living and what each person is feeling. Then, read through the Discussion Questions and consider what you would like to change about your body language and attire.

Figure 1

Figure 2

Figure 3

Figure 4

Figure 5

Figure 6

4

Getting to Know You

Games for Building Rapport with Customers

Alphabet Improv

In a Nutshell

In this variation of a popular party game, salespeople have a spontaneous conversation by beginning each statement with a particular letter of the alphabet. This game is very unpredictable and always fun. It stimulates quick thinking and helps salespeople to develop conversation and rapport-building skills. It's suitable for all salespeople.

Time

5–10 minutes.

What You'll Need

Nothing!

What to Do

Divide the group into pairs and ask them to decide who'll play the "salesperson" and who'll play the "customer." (After one round, they'll switch roles.)

Tell salespeople to imagine they're in a sales setting. (Note: You may want to elaborate on this by giving them fictional products or services to represent—dental supplies, interior decorating services, etc.) Their job is to have a conversation following this one rule: The salesperson starts by making a statement starting with the letter A. Then the customer responds with a statement starting with the letter B. They must continue until they've reached Z.

Example:

Salesperson: All next week, our products will be on sale.
Customer: Bet that will be a busy week!....

Encourage salespeople to play quickly and spontaneously rather than to think too much about what to say.

Hidden Rapport

In a Nutshell

This is a quick, active game in which participants work together on a find-a-word puzzle to uncover a variety of techniques for building rapport with customers. Plan to conduct this game before rather than after the other games in this chapter (once participants have done the other games, they'll know the answers to the puzzle). This game is ideal for new hires, but it can be used as a refresher for employees at all levels.

Time

10–15 minutes.

What You'll Need

One copy of the handout on page 55 for each pair of participants.

What to Do

Ask someone to define "rapport." Divide the participants into pairs and tell them they'll be working with their partners to uncover several techniques for building rapport with customers.

Hand out the puzzle and give them about ten minutes to complete it. Go over the answers as a group.

Answers

1. Use the customer's NAME.

2. Say PLEASE and THANK YOU when asking customers for INFORMATION.

3. Explain your REASONS when you have to say NO to a customer's request.

4. Show your INTEREST in the customer's needs.

5. Show EMPATHY for the customer's FEELINGS.

6. Let the customer know what his or her OPTIONS are.

7. SMILE! Even if you're on the phone!

If You're on Your Own

Follow the instructions on page 55 and complete the puzzle. Be sure you're using all these rapport-building techniques during your sales day.

Rapport Puzzle

There are countless ways to build rapport with customers. The puzzle below contains words that complete the following rapport-building techniques. We've done the first one for you.

1. Use the customer's <u>N</u> <u>A</u> <u>M</u> <u>E</u>.
2. Say _ _ _ _ _ _ and _ _ _ _ _ _ _ _ _ when asking customers for
    _ _ _ _ _ _ _ _ _ _ _ _.
3. Explain your _ _ _ _ _ _ _ _ when you have to say _ _ to a customer's request.
4. Show your _ _ _ _ _ _ _ _ _ in the customer's needs.
5. Show _ _ _ _ _ _ _ _ for the customer's _ _ _ _ _ _ _ _ _.
6. Let the customer know what his or her _ _ _ _ _ _ _ _ are.
7. _ _ _ _ _! Even if you're on the phone!

Words can appear horizontally, vertically, or diagonally, and may go in any direction.

R	M	I	I	K	S	L	E	R	S	T
O	P	M	K	Y	R	E	J	S	W	E
O	T	R	E	E	L	C	N	H	E	E
T	H	A	N	K	Y	O	U	A	S	M
S	E	R	R	A	S	P	B	G	A	P
E	M	A	N	A	A	T	N	M	E	A
R	D	I	E	L	D	I	A	P	L	T
E	Q	R	L	O	L	O	W	I	P	H
T	I	R	E	E	O	N	N	U	Y	Y
N	O	W	E	R	H	S	A	E	L	P
I	N	F	O	R	M	A	T	I	O	N

Small Talk

In a Nutshell

Salespeople learn to pick up clues from potential buyers that can help them to build a strong rapport. This game is designed for salespeople in the face-to-face sales environment and is especially helpful for those who have difficulty making light, easy conversation with customers.

Note: This game should be played by salespeople who are familiar with the concept of rapport.

Time

10–15 minutes.

What You'll Need

Prepare for this game by cutting out of magazines photographs of people in everyday life situations (you'll need seven to ten photos for each group of participants). The people in the photographs should not be famous or recognizable. By combing a variety of publications, you should be able to find a diverse representation of fictional customers.

Tip! After the game, collect the photographs and keep them on file for future use. You can add to the collection as you come across interesting photographs in magazines.

What to Do

Briefly discuss the concept of rapport. Tell salespeople that in this game they will practice picking up clues from customers that can help them build a strong rapport.

Divide the salespeople into groups of two or three. Give each group a selection of "customer" photographs and ask them to study the photos and come up with statements they might use to make pleasant, light conversation with customers. Each statement should have some relevance to the photograph. Give them an example by holding up a photo and suggesting two or three statements you might make to the customer.

Let's say, for example, you had a photo of a man in a Denver Broncos shirt with three children in tow. You might say:

- *How old are your children?*
- *Are you a Broncos fan?*
- *Sounds as if you all had quite a winter in Denver this year!*

After about ten minutes, ask the groups to share one or two of their photos and accompanying statements with the rest of the participants.

If You're on Your Own

Collect pictures from magazines. Work with a friend or family member to develop statements you might use to start a conversation with the person in the picture.

Well, If He Can Do It . . .

In a Nutshell

Participants read a case study of a sales interaction in which the employee did a great job. They have to identify what the sales representative did to build a strong rapport with the customer. This game is suitable for all salespeople who need to learn to develop rapport with customers.

Time

10–15 minutes.

What You'll Need

One copy of the handouts on pages 63 and 64 for each salesperson.

What to Do

Give one copy of the handout on page 63 to each sales-person and ask them to read it.

Review the handout on page 64 with salespeople. Ask them to work in groups of two or three to review the scenario on page 63 and underline the passages that show what the sales representative said to build a good rapport with the customer.

Review each group's answers and discuss as needed.

Ask participants to keep a copy of page 64 at their workstations until they've mastered the skill of building rapport.

FRIENDLY FRAN: *(Greeting the customer with a friendly smile and a warm handshake)* Thank you for coming in today. My name is Fran. How may I help you today?

TRAVELIN' TRAVIS: I have this coupon I clipped out of the Sunday paper for a round-trip flight from Dallas to London for $447. It's on Atlas Air, but I wanted to check to see if there's another airline that has a better fare. I'm also a frequent flyer with Global Village, and I'd like to get the miles for the trip if they can beat that fare.

FRIENDLY FRAN: I'm glad you came in. Have a seat right here and I'll be happy to check our lowest fare to London. That's a lot of miles! When are you planning to travel?

TRAVELIN' TRAVIS: In April, around the 15th.

FRIENDLY FRAN: What a nice time to go to London! Let me check with Global Village and see what they have available. . . . Well, if you leave on a Sunday, Monday, or Tuesday—that would be the 16th, 17th, or 18th—and return on one of those days as well, we can get you a direct flight to Heathrow airport for $515 round-trip. That's our Spring Special fare. Would you like me to make you a reservation? We can hold it at no obligation for 24 hours. That gives you some time to think about what will work best for you.

TRAVELIN' TRAVIS: $515, huh? That's quite a bit more than Atlas's fare, but I *would* like to take a direct flight. Sure, go ahead and reserve a space for me. The name's Jones—Travis Jones.

FRIENDLY FRAN: Great, I hope this works for you. I can book you on the morning flight, which would put you into London in the early evening, or you can take the night flight and arrive at 8 a.m. Which would you prefer, Mr. Jones?

Techniques for Building Rapport

All sales representatives have the opportunity to build rapport in every interaction with the customer. Although there's no "right" formula for building rapport, there are a few simple techniques that can be helpful:

1. Smile.

2. Make eye contact.

3. Use the customer's name.

4. Say "please" and "thank you."

5. Explain your reasons for saying no.

6. Show your interest in the customer's needs.

7. Be empathetic to the customer's feelings.

8. Let the customer know his or her options.

To Each His Own

In a Nutshell

In this activity, salespeople examine their own preferences for business interactions (including sales situations) and compare them with the preferences of their customers. The objective of the activity is for salespeople to learn that it is easy to customize a sales presentation to individual buyers. This activity is suitable for salespeople at all levels.

Time

20–30 minutes.

What You'll Need

One copy of the overhead on page 67. One copy of the handout on page 68 for each participant.

What to Do

Review the overhead. Explain that some people are more relationship-oriented and some people are more task-oriented; some people prefer to get to know people by socializing with them and others prefer to get to know people by working on a project with them. Ask participants to make a mental mark on the *y*-axis as to where they fall in this continuum.

Then explain that some people are fast-paced and others are slow-paced; some people move quickly, speak quickly, and make decisions quickly, whereas others move and speak more slowly and are more analytical or cautious in making a decision. Ask participants to make a mental mark on the x-axis as to where they fall on this continuum. Then have participants put themselves into one quadrant, based on their two marks.

Ask them to consider someone they get along with very well and determine which quadrant that person belongs to; then have them do the same with someone they find difficult. Discuss the results.

Distribute the handout and give participants a few moments to review it. Explain that there is no right or wrong quadrant; each quadrant has its positive and negative aspects. Point out that the problem arises when a person from one quadrant enters a business transaction with a person from another quadrant, particularly if the people are in diametrically opposed quadrants.

For example, a Q1 customer may feel that a Q3 salesperson is overly aggressive—just because the Q3 representative gets right down to business. Or a Q2 customer may feel that a Q4 salesperson doesn't care about building a long-term relationship.

Ask participants to think about some of their current and potential customers. How can they adapt their sales presentations to put the buyer at ease?

Relationship-oriented

Slow-
paced

Fast-
paced

Task-oriented

Relationship-oriented

Q1

- Likes to talk about family, friends, activities, and other personal information
- Appreciates your taking time to develop a personal relationship or a business "friendship"
- Likes to be given information verbally—preferably face-to-face
- Doesn't like to be pushed into making quick decisions

Q2

- Likes to tell stories based on personal experience
- Will take time to develop a personal relationship or a business "friendship" with you
- Doesn't want a lot of detail—just key facts
- Tends to make decisions quickly based in large part on personal relationships

Slow-paced

Fast-paced

Q4

- Prefers talking about the business situation at hand rather than making small talk
- Likes to have lots of back-up data
- Doesn't like to be pushed into making quick decisions
- Tends to analyze all the details before making a decision

Q3

- Wants to get down to business quickly
- Is more interested in completing the transaction than in becoming your friend
- May ask lots of questions; you feel like you're being "grilled"
- Tends to make decisions quickly based on the facts—likes written summaries of key points

Task-oriented

5

Target Practice

Games for Identifying Buyer Needs

The One-Minute Customer

In a Nutshell

Salespeople create composites of fictional customers and then work in teams to brainstorm as many customer needs as they can in one minute. This game is particularly helpful for expanding creativity and "thinking outside the box." It's suitable for all salespeople.

Time

5–10 minutes.

What You'll Need

Several pieces of flip-chart paper and some marker pens. Prepare each flip-chart page with the following information (keep the information on the top half of the page):

Customer name:
Hometown:
Age:
Occupation:
Hobbies:
Family status:

What to Do

Divide salespeople into teams of two or three and give each team one piece of flip-chart paper and a marker pen.

Without giving away the object of the game, tell each team to create a "customer" by filling in the information for each category. Encourage them to create interesting characters. Allow one minute for this step.

Now tell the teams to brainstorm as many customer needs as they can in one minute, based on the information they've come up with for their "customer." For example, if you sell clothing and the customer lives in Minneapolis, he would need a winter coat.

After one minute, ask the teams to read out their flip-charts to the group. Give a small reward to the team that came up with the most customer needs in the time provided.

Amateur Architects

In a Nutshell

This is a lengthy but popular game in which salespeople learn to use open and closed questions strategically. Their objective is to draw a house as described by their partners. This game is excellent for helping both new and experienced salespeople improve their questioning skills.

Time

30–40 minutes.

What You'll Need

Overhead transparencies or flip-charts of the information on pages 76 and 77. One copy of the "House A" handout on page 78 for half the salespeople, one copy of the "House B" handout on page 79 for half the salespeople. Blank paper and pens or pencils.

What to Do

Use the information on pages 76 and 77 to explain the difference between open and closed questions.

Put salespeople into pairs and explain that the object of the game is for one participant to draw a house that matches the house his or her partner will be given. Salespeople who are drawing can ask any questions they want and as many as they want in five minutes. Salespeople who are describing the house should follow the instructions on the handout.

Distribute the "House A" handout to the salespeople who will be describing the house; hand out a sheet of blank paper to the salespeople who will be drawing. Ask partners to sit back-to-back, and spread salespeople out so that those drawing cannot see the houses of those who are describing.

After five minutes, have the describer and drawer compare houses. Debrief the game. Point out how open questions tend to solicit more general information than closed questions.

Have pairs switch roles. Distribute the "House B" handout to the salespeople who will be describing the house; hand out a blank sheet of paper to the salespeople who will be drawing.

After five minutes, have the describer and drawer compare houses and debrief the game.

Discussion Questions

Q: What types of questions work best when you want specific information?

A: *Closed questions.*

Q: What types of questions work best when you want the prospect to speak freely?

A: *Open questions.*

A: Q: What types of questions work best when you need to gather information about your prospect's needs?

A: *A combination. Open questions get more information to start with, but when you need specifics, you need to use closed questions.*

Q: How does this game relate to your job as a salesperson?

A: *Field answers.*

If You Have More Time

Develop a list of open and closed questions salespeople can use to gather information from their customers to help them better understand and meet customer needs.

Open Questions

- Solicit more than a "yes" or "no" or other one-word response.

- Aim to get someone talking.

- Are useful when you want general information.

- Use common lead-ins such as what, how, and why.

Closed Questions

- Solicit a "yes" or "no" or other one-word response.

- Aim to limit talking or to control direction of conversation.

- Are useful when you want specific information.

- Use common lead-ins such as who, when, did, which, would, are, can, have, do, is, will, and may.

House "A"

Answer questions about the house as asked. If your partner asks you an open question, describe several features about the house. If your partner asks a closed question, only give a "yes," "no," or short reply. Do not volunteer information.

House "B"

Answer questions about the house as asked. If your partner asks you an open question, describe several features about the house. If your partner asks a closed question, only give a "yes," "no," or short reply. Do not volunteer information.

What the World Needs Now

In a Nutshell

Salespeople work together to come up with ways in which their products contribute toward universal human needs. This game increases salespeople's confidence in their products, and it gives them practice in quick and creative thinking. The game is suitable for all salespeople.

Time

10–15 minutes

What You'll Need

An overhead or flip-chart of the information on page 83. Flip-chart and markers. Salespeople will need paper and pens.

What to Do

Begin the game by asking participants to brainstorm other needs to add to the list. Write them on the overhead transparency or flip-chart as the group announces them. Don't spend more than a minute or so on this portion of the game.

Divide the salespeople into groups of two or three, and instruct them to discuss the ways in which their products contribute toward these universal needs. If the salespeople represent a variety of products, you may want to assign each group different products to discuss. Use the following example as a model of how to play the game.

Product: XJ 337 Scanner
Gives people peace of mind because it's well-made and simple to use. Helps keep the environment clean by eliminating excess paper......

Encourage salespeople to think creatively and to be cautious of discarding ideas as insignificant.

After five or ten minutes, reconvene the salespeople and ask each group to share their insights.

If You're on Your Own

Take a minute or two to add needs to the list on page 83, and then consider how your product or products contribute toward these needs. Write your insights on a piece of paper, and keep it for future reference.

What the World Needs Now

- Peace of mind

- A clean environment

- An end to violence

- Universal good health

-

-

-

-

-

6

What's That You Say?

Games to Improve Listening Skills

I'm All Ears

In a Nutshell

Salespeople assess their own listening skills and habits. This is an ideal introduction to a training session on listening or communication skills.

Time

5–10 minutes.

What You'll Need

One copy of the handouts on pages 89 and 90 for each salesperson.

What to Do

Give the two handouts to each salesperson. Give them a few minutes to complete the assessments and to come up with an action plan for improving their listening habits.

End the activity by holding a brief discussion about the importance of listening in the sales environment. What can be gained from good listening? What can be lost due to poor listening? Do any of the salespeople have stories about their own experiences of listening or not listening to their buyers?

If You're on Your Own

Complete the two listening assessments and come up with an action plan for improving your listening habits.

Are You All Ears?

Some people are good listeners while others are not. Most of us fall somewhere in the middle—we're good listeners in some situations, with some people, when discussing some topics. Take a moment now to evaluate your listening skills. How do you believe the following people would rate you—on a scale of 1 to 5—as a listener? (5 = best)

Yourself   _____

Your customers   _____

Your spouse   _____

Your boss   _____

Your co-workers   _____

Your best friend   _____

Now add the scores together and plot the total on the listening spectrum.

5	10	15	20	25	30

Brick Wall   *The Human Ear*

Are You All Ears?

Review the following list of poor listening habits and mark each with an "F" (frequently), "S" (sometimes), or "R" (rarely) according to how often you exhibit the tendency:

_____ I pretend I'm paying attention when my mind is drifting off.

_____ I cut people off or finish their sentences because I know what they're going to say.

_____ When someone is speaking to me, I look around the room to see what else is happening.

_____ I shuffle papers on my desk or start doing some other task when someone talks too long or too slowly.

_____ When someone is speaking, I plan what I will say next.

_____ When a person speaks too fast or uses words I don't understand, I let it go and listen only for what I do understand.

What can you do during the upcoming week to improve your listening skills?

_____

_____

_____

The Listening Quiz

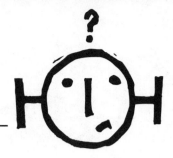

In a Nutshell

This fun game reminds salespeople of the importance of listening in the sales process. It's suitable for salespeople at all levels.

Time

5–10 minutes.

What You'll Need

Each salesperson will need paper and a pen.

What to Do

Hold a brief discussion about the role of listening in the sales process.

Ask the participants to take out a sheet of paper. Tell them to print their name in the top left hand corner of the sheet, and explain that you'll read ten questions. Their job is to listen, to write down the question number, and to write the answer to the question. Let them know that you'll only read each question once and they may not take notes. This quiz will serve as an assessment of their listening skills.

When you're ready, begin the questions. Go through all the questions before you come back to discuss their answers.

1. You need to travel to trade shows in California, Florida, Wisconsin, South Dakota, and Maryland. Which of these states contains the letter F?

    California and Florida

2. You work for "Big P" food distributor. You sell potatoes, potato chips, pretzels, pop, peanuts, popsicles, and posies and you promise next-day delivery. On Thursday, your customer faxed in an order for pop, peanuts, popcorn, and potatoes. True or false. You'll be able to deliver this complete order on Friday.

    False. You don't sell popcorn.

3. You sell various types of rides to amusement parks and carnivals. The ferris wheels in your product line have catalog item numbers of F-443, F-1668, F-235, F-126, and F-37. How many catalog items have four numerical digits?

    One. The F-1668.

4. How do you say J-O-K-E? (Ask for verbal response)

   How do you say P-O-K-E? (Ask for verbal response)

   How do you say B-L-O-K-E? (Ask for verbal response)

   How do you say S-M-O-K-E? (Ask for verbal response)

   Write down what you call the white of an egg.

   Albumen or egg white. The white of an egg is not the yolk. Point out the importance of not having any expectations while listening.

5. You sell class rings and graduation invitations. While exhibiting your wares on campus one day, several students placed orders. The first one was Susan, then Johnny, Penny, Malcolm, Larry, and Amy. Who was the third student to place an order?

   Penny.

6. You sell irrigation equipment to farmers. Farmer Fred in Omaha said that he had an acre square of land that needed to be irrigated. Farmer Frank in Tulsa said he had a square acre that needed to be irrigated. True or false? Their property is the same size and shape, and you can sell them both the exact same irrigation system.

   False. Although the area may be the same, there may be a difference in shape. An acre square is square. A square acre may be square, it may be long and thin, or it may be broken into parcels. Point out the importance of listening carefully and transcending your own frame of reference.

7. You sell fruit to fruit stands. During your calls today, Mr. Cherry bought some oranges, Mrs. Lemon bought some pears, Mr. Fig bought some apples, Mrs. Kiwi bought some grapes, and Mrs. Berry bought some bananas. Who bought the pears?

Mrs. Lemon

Debrief the activity by discussing how listening also involves retaining information, not having expectations about the message, and not being limited by your own frame of reference. Ask how many salespeople would have found this game easier if they had been able to take notes, and point out that listening can be greatly improved by the simple act of taking notes.

As a final note, ask which participants <u>printed</u> their name in the upper <u>left</u> hand corner of their paper, as you had asked.

If You're on Your Own

Ask a friend or family member to read the instructions on page 91, then read the listening quiz as you take it.

So What You're Saying Is . . .

In a Nutshell

This activity teaches salespeople to confirm their understanding of a prospect's or customer's statement or request. It is a good activity to use if your salespeople frequently make presentations without thoroughly understanding the customer's situation and needs.

Time

10–15 minutes.

What You'll Need

One copy of the handout on page 98 for each salesperson. Blank paper for taking notes.

What to Do

Review the steps for confirming understanding from the handout on page 98.

Hand out a blank sheet of paper to each salesperson. Tell them that you will be reading some customer statements. Their job is to take notes of the key facts they hear and then use the four steps of confirming listed on the handout to confirm their understanding of your statement. When they have a confirming statement ready, they should stand up.

Read the following statements and ask the first few salespeople who stand up to read their confirming statements.

1. I'm interested in bringing a group to the zoo on April 10. There will be ten children, four adults over eighteen, and four senior citizens. Two of the adults are students. Do you have special discounts for students and senior citizens? Or a group discount?

2. I want to get a computer for my daughter for a holiday gift. It should have all the right software for her age—she's nine—but I don't know what that is. And, well, I don't know what I should spend or what type I should buy. I can't afford a lot, but I want to get something that will work for her.

3. They come in green, red, and blue? OK. I want 24—one dozen of each.

4. I've had a checking account and a savings account with your bank for the past few years. I've just turned 55, and now I don't know if I'm supposed to be in the Senior Gold Account or if I should stay in the standard account. Actually, my wife said we might be better off. We don't have many checks we write each month.

If You Have More Time

Put salespeople in pairs. One salesperson will develop a complex statement that would be heard on the job; the other salesperson will practice confirming his or her understanding. Then have them switch roles and do it again.

If You're on Your Own

Make a copy of page 98 and keep it in front of you as you develop confirming statements for the customer statements on page 96. Write two or three statements for each scenario.

Confirming Your Understanding

Step 1   Use a confirming statement.

> Let me confirm...
> Let me make sure I understand your request...
> So you want...
> I'd just like to confirm that...

Step 2   Summarize key facts.

> You want to compare benefits for hospital stays.
> You'd like to find out if floor seats are available.
> You're concerned about the price.

Step 3   Ask if your understanding is correct.

> Did I get that right?
> Is that correct?
> Did I understand you correctly?
> Right?
> Is that it?

Step 4   Clarify misunderstandings (if necessary).

Feelings

In a Nutshell

This game focuses on dealing with buyer feelings. In it, some salespeople play the role of buyer and exhibit a pre-selected feeling while another salesperson is making a presentation. The rest of the group determines how the salesperson might adopt his or her presentation to deal with the buyer's feelings.

Time

20–30 minutes.

What You'll Need

A flip-chart and marker pens.

What to Do

Discuss the role of a buyer's feelings in determining the outcome of a sales presentation. Ask salespeople for various feelings their buyers might exhibit that might influence their sales presentation. Post the responses on a flip-chart. (Some examples might be skeptical, excited, distant, distracted.)

Ask for a few volunteers to play the part of a buyer and for a few to play the part of a salesperson. Ask each buyer to review the flip-chart and select a feeling to portray.

Ask each salesperson to prepare a brief product presentation. As the salesperson greets the buyer and begins his or her presentation, the buyer should communicate his or her feeling through body language as well as words and tone.

Tell both the buyer and the salesperson to have some fun with their roles. This does not need to be a formal and serious presentation.

After two to three minutes, stop the presentation and ask the group the following questions:

1. What feeling was the buyer exhibiting?

2. What did the buyer say or do that conveyed that feeling?

3. What might the salesperson do during the rest of the presentation to take into consideration the buyer's feelings? (For example, if the buyer was skeptical, the salesperson could offer proof of his or her claims.)

If You're on Your Own

After each sales call this week, take a moment to identify the buyer's feelings. When you've developed a list of feelings, work on your own or with another salesperson to brainstorm ways of identifying those feelings and dealing with them during your presentations.

7

It Slices, It Dices!

Games for Presentation Success

What I Mean Is . . .

In a Nutshell

Salespeople focus on identifying words and terms that qualify as jargon or slang. This fast-paced team game helps salespeople at all levels of experience become more aware of both common and unusual jargon terms.

Time

15–20 minutes.

What You'll Need

An overhead transparency of the information on page 107, or the definitions copied onto a flip-chart or white board. Salespeople will need paper and pens.

What to Do

Go over the definitions of jargon and slang to make sure everyone knows what they are.

Divide the salespeople into teams of two or three. Tell each team to designate one member as the player and another as the recorder. If you divide the group into teams of three, the third member can be a coach to the player, or two players can take turns.

Tell the group that you'll read out several statements from salespeople in a variety of fields. They should listen carefully to each statement and then follow these directions:

- If the team hears a jargon term they don't understand, the player should stand up and put one hand on his or her head.
- If the team hears a jargon term that they do understand (it's still jargon), the player should put one hand on his or her stomach.
- If the team hears slang, the player should stand on one leg.

Warn salespeople that each statement may require them to take one, two, or even all three of the positions.

Read the statements out loud, one at a time. Read each statement two times at a normal pace. Give teams a few moments to confer and to take their positions (the recorder should write down the slang and jargon terms). Then call on one team to identify the slang and jargon terms and to say why they took the positions they did. The game should be lively and lighthearted.

Tip! You can enhance this game by including some jargon specific to your company or industry. If possible, take some time before playing the game to write some typical jargon-laden statements that salespeople might use in conversations with customers. Add these statements to those on page 105.

"What I Mean Is . . ." Statements

Jargon and slang terms are underlined.

1. How many <u>meg</u> do you want on your hard drive?

2. Are you interested in the <u>Super Saver</u> account or the <u>Max Plus</u> account?

3. Your system comes with some <u>snap extras</u>: track ball, surge suppressor, glare filter.

4. Just fill out this form, mark your <u>DOB</u>, and give us your <u>ATF</u> and your <u>remit</u>. It's <u>no sweat.</u>

5. With this type of coverage, you're responsible for all <u>copayments</u> and your <u>PAD</u>, <u>CYD</u>, and <u>PDD</u> deductibles. We'll pick up the rest.

6. Once you've completed all the documentation, we'll calculate your <u>points</u>. Then we'll figure in your <u>down</u>, and find out if you're eligible for the loan.

7. <u>Gotcha</u>! You need a <u>1442 LX</u> and 4 cases of paper. Do you want that to be regular paper or our special <u>Laser Deluxe</u>?

If You're on Your Own

Make a product presentation to a few friends or family members who aren't overly familiar with your product or industry. Give them a pen and paper and ask them to write down any slang you use as well as any terms they don't understand.

Review the terms they wrote. Unless you're sure your buyer will understand these terms, eliminate them from your presentations or make a point to explain them. For example, you might refer to the paper in statement 7 on page 105 as "Laser Deluxe—that's our premium paper. It's specially designed to prevent the curling that occurs when regular paper passes through a laser printer."

jargon (jahr' gun) n. vocabulary specific to a particular trade or profession

Examples: chem 7   (a medical test)

drop ship   (a method of delivering products to buyers)

four top   (a restaurant table for four people)

slang (slang) n. informal usage in vocabulary that is characteristically more metaphorical, vivid, and playful than ordinary language

Examples: buttery   (nice)

flame   (use e-mail to write disparagingly about someone)

Yo!   (a greeting)

Toy with Success

In a Nutshell

Salespeople focus on presenting product benefits to customers by selecting a toy from a box and convincing the class to buy their toy.

Time

15–20 minutes.

What You'll Need

An overhead transparency or flip-chart of the information on page 170. A box filled with children's toys. Blank paper for participants to write benefits when they hear them. A stopwatch.

What to Do

Review the overhead with salespeople and point out the importance of presenting benefits during a sales presentation.

Ask salespeople to select a toy from the toy box. Their job is to make a one-minute, benefit-rich sales presentation with the objective of convincing the audience to purchase their toy.

Hand out the blank paper. During presentations, the rest of the group listens for benefits and jots them down on the paper. At the end of each presentation, ask the group how many benefits they heard.

Give salespeople two minutes to prepare their presentation, then begin the game. Give a small prize or other award to the salesperson who gave the greatest number of benefits during his or her presentation.

Colors

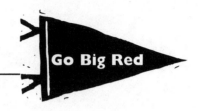

Go Big Red

In a Nutshell

Salespeople practice their presentation and persuasion skills by competing with one another to win over the "buyers." The catch is that the products are nothing more than colors—red, green, blue, yellow, etc. This game is best suited to experienced salespeople who are adept at making spontaneous presentations and who are comfortable "competing" with others.

Time

Approximately 20 minutes; time will vary depending on the number of presentations.

What You'll Need

One copy of page 113. Paper, pen, tape. A clock or watch with a second hand or digital timer.

What to Do

Make a copy of page 113 and cut along the dotted lines. While the salespeople are out of the room, tape one color to the bottom of each person's chair.

Set up the game by telling the salespeople that they'll be competing with one another by making brief presentations. The object is to get the "audience" (the other participants) to select their product. After all the presentations, the group will vote on who was the most persuasive.

Tell them they'll have five minutes to prepare for their presentations and a maximum of one minute to present. Finally, let the salespeople know that they'll each be making a presentation of a color—an intangible product. They can say or do whatever they want to in order to get the audience to choose their color over someone else's.

Once they understand what they're supposed to do, tell them to look under their chairs and begin preparing. After five minutes, ask someone to make the first one-minute presentation. Continue until everyone has had a turn, and then hold a vote to determine the winner.

Spend a few minutes debriefing the game by discussing what was effective, and how this can be carried over to the real-time sales environment.

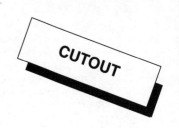
Red	Orange
Yellow	Purple
Green	Brown
Black	Grey
Blue	Tan
White	Pink

When You Have to Say No

In a Nutshell

Salespeople learn what to do when they have to say "no" to a buyer by role-playing salespeople who are unable to fulfill buyers' requests. This activity is suitable for salespeople of all levels—particularly those who need to deliver bad news to customers.

Time

15–20 minutes.

What You'll Need

An overhead transparency or a flip-chart of the information on page 118. One copy of the instructions on page 119 for each salesperson. Copies of role play #1 on pages 120 and 121 for half the number of salespeople in the group. Copies of role play #2 on pages 122 and 123 for half the number of salespeople in the group.

What to Do

Discuss the fact that there are times when salespeople won't be able to meet every buyer's request. For example, the buyer may want a product or service that their company doesn't offer or a product that is out of stock.

When the salesperson can't meet the buyer's needs or when the salesperson has to deliver bad news, it's important to remember to do three things. *Review the overhead transparency or flip-chart.*

1. Show empathy
2. Explain the reason (if applicable)
3. Tell the buyer what you <u>can</u> do

Give salespeople an example, then leave the overhead projector on or the flip-chart posted in the room.

Let the group know that they'll be participating in two quick, fun role plays where they can practice these skills. Divide the group into pairs and give each salesperson a copy of the instructions on page 119. Review the instructions with the group.

Hand out the salesperson role for Role Play #1 to one person in each pair. Hand out the buyer role for Role Play #1 to the other person in each pair. Give them a few moments to review their roles. Remind them that they can refer to the steps listed on the overhead or flip-chart.

Answer any questions, then begin the role plays. They should only take two to three minutes including feedback.

Debrief the first round of role plays, then ask participants to switch roles. Hand out the salesperson role for Role Play #2 to the person who played the buyer during the first role play. Hand out the buyer's role for Role Play #2 to the person who played the salesperson during the first role play. Give participants a few minutes to review their role, then begin the second round of role plays. Debrief the role play after two to three minutes.

If You Have More Time

Ask salespeople to come up with situations where they have to turn down a buyer's request or deliver bad news. Capture answers on a flip-chart or white board. Divide the salespeople into groups of three to four and assign one or two of the situations to each group. Ask them to refer to the steps listed on the overhead or flip-chart and develop statements they can make to buyers to present their negative news in a more positive light.

If You're on Your Own

Develop a list of situations where you have to turn down buyers' requests or deliver bad news. Refer to the steps listed on page 118 and develop statements for each situation that you can use to present this negative news in a more positive light.

When You Have to Say No

1. **Show empathy**

2. **Explain the reason (if necessary)**

3. **Tell the buyer what you <u>can</u> do**

Instructions

When you're the salesperson . . .

1. Read the entire page before beginning the role play.

2. Greet the buyer using the statement printed on your scenario sheet.

3. Respond to the buyer's request using the information on your scenario sheet.

4. Refer to the steps posted in the room and use the appropriate steps for saying no.

5. The buyer will inform you when the role play has ended.

When you're the Buyer . . .

1. Read the entire page before beginning the role play.

2. After the salesperson greets you, respond with your first statement.

3. Continue until the salesperson has given you all the information you've requested.

4. Follow the instructions on your scenario sheet for ending the role play.

5. Briefly give feedback on the salesperson's performance based on the information on your scenario sheet.

How to Give Feedback

Discuss the role play with the salesperson and congratulate him or her on the steps that were carried out correctly. If the salesperson didn't respond to your request using the appropriate skills, briefly point out what should have been done, according to your copy of the handout. Remember, it's important to be supportive, encouraging, and honest when giving feedback to a peer.

Salesperson's Role #1

You're a field salesperson for Food Systems, Inc., a large wholesaler of food and other restaurant supplies.

Here's what you can do:

- Offer a product line of more than 4,000 items
- Arrange a 20-day Preferred Customer payment schedule upon credit approval
- Guarantee delivery by 9 a.m.

Here's what you cannot do:

- Provide dairy, produce, or other fresh supplies
- Offer payment terms longer than 20 days
- Guarantee early morning delivery

Greet the buyer by saying, "Good morning, my name is <your name> with Food Systems, Inc. Thanks for calling to set up this appointment. How can I help you today?"

The buyer will let you know when the sales call is over.

FOOD SYSTEMS, INC.

Buyer Role #1

You own a restaurant and you called Food Systems, Inc. to set up an appointment for a salesperson to visit you to discuss their wholesale food services. When the salesperson greets you, say, **"I'm looking for a new supplier for our restaurant. Do you carry produce as well as dry goods?"**

> *The salesperson should let you know that they don't supply produce, but do have a product line of over 4,000 items.*

After the salesperson has answered your first question, say, **"We do all our cooking in the morning, so we usually need supplies by around 7 or 8. Can you deliver by then?"**

> *The salesperson should tell you that they can guarantee delivery by 9 a.m.*

After the salesperson explains their delivery schedule, say, **"Well, that would probably work. Just one more thing—I pay the large bills once a month. Can you arrange 30-day payment terms?"**

> *The salesperson should offer to arrange a 20-day payment schedule upon credit approval.*

Once your questions have been answered, end the role play by saying, **"Thank you. I'll take a look at the books and give you a call if that will work."**

Critique:
When turning down your requests, did the salesperson use the steps listed?

FOOD SYSTEMS, INC.

Salesperson's Role #2

You're an inside sales representative at QuickNet, an Internet access provider.

Here's what you can do:

- Offer an introductory rate of $49 for the first three months (Service is $20 per month after that.)

- Offer online technical support (via e-mail) and a four-hour turnaround on technical support calls via telephone

- Send out the software installation package via overnight delivery

Here's what you cannot do:

- Offer a free trial subscription

- Give immediate technical support over the telephone

- Connect them to the Internet before they've installed the software

Greet the caller by saying, "Good afternoon, QuickNet. This is <your name>. How may I help you?"

The caller will let you know when the sales call is over.

Buyer Role #2

You're calling QuickNet, an Internet access provider. When the salesperson greets you, say, **"I'd like to get Internet access and I heard about one company offering a free ten-day trial. Do you do that?"**

The salesperson should tell you no, and let you know about their introductory offer.

After the salesperson explains the introductory offer, say, **"Well, what if I have questions once I've set up the connection? Do you have a help line that's always open?"**

The salesperson should tell you how to get technical support.

After the salesperson explains how to get technical support, say, **"Well, it sounds pretty good. Can you just hook me up right now? My modem number is 805-555-6723."**

The salesperson should let you know that you must install software first, and should offer to send it to you.

When the salesperson has answered your questions, end the practice call by saying, **"It sounds good. Let me get my credit card and I'll call you back."**

Critique:
When turning down your requests, did the salesperson use the steps listed?

Dressing for Success

In a Nutshell

This is a consciousness-raising game for salespeople at all levels. Participants examine their own biases and impressions based on people's appearances, and then discuss what impressions buyers might have of them, based on their appearance.

Time

10–15 minutes.

What You'll Need

Select several (at least five per group) photographs of people from magazines or print advertisements. The photographs should represent as diverse a population as possible. The photos should not portray famous or recognizable people.

What to Do

Divide salespeople into groups of three or four and give each group several photographs to examine. Tell them to discuss among themselves what impressions they have of these people based solely on how they look in the photograph.

After about five minutes, ask for some volunteers to briefly report each group's impressions. Then tell them to think about and discuss what impressions buyers might have of them (the salespeople) based on how they look.

Emphasize that the objective of this game is not to debate whether or not these first impressions are fair. The salespeople should focus solely on what impression their appearance makes on potential buyers.

Tip! Keep the magazine pictures in a file for future use. You can add to the file whenever you come across appropriate photographs in magazines.

You might like to mention that it's been suggested by experts that employees should always dress as if they held a job one level above their current status. This makes a favorable impression on customers and on managers, and it may help them win consideration for promotions.

If You're on Your Own

The next time you read a magazine, look at photographs of people in articles and in ads. What impressions do you have of these people based on how they look?

Dress as you do for a typical sales meeting. Take a look in the mirror. What impression do you have of the person in the mirror? Is it the impression you want your customers to have of you? If not, what do you need to change for customers to have a more favorable impression?

If you like shopping, here's another idea. Spend an hour or two at your favorite clothing stores. Try on a variety of outfits suitable for business and assign three adjectives to each "look"—frumpy, powerful, fun, etc.

8

Sales Solutions

Games for Problem Solving

Ticket for Success

In a Nutshell

In this activity, salespeople help each other solve current sales problems. It is suitable for all salespeople, even new ones who can lend a fresh perspective to sales situations.

Time

10–15 minutes.

What You'll Need

One copy of the handout on page 133 for each salesperson.

What to Do

Hand out a copy of page 133 to each salesperson before the session begins. Tell the salesperson to read the instructions, complete the handout, and bring it to the session. It will serve as their "admission ticket."

When salespeople are gathered for the game, instruct them to pass their "ticket" to the person on their left. Each salesperson will now have a "ticket" with another salesperson's problem on it. Give salespeople 20–30 seconds to consider the problem, and write a solution on the back of the form. After 20–30 seconds holler "Show Time," which will serve as an indication that salespeople should pass the ticket to the person on their left.

Continue in this fashion until each salesperson has his or her own form back. Give them a few moments to review the solutions on the back of the form; then conclude the session.

If You're on Your Own

Create a list of your three biggest sales problems. Ask for advice from a friend or a salesperson in another industry. Even though they may not thoroughly understand your selling environment, their input may spark an idea that will help you see the problem in a fresh light and find a solution.

Ticket to Success

Instructions:

Consider a sales problem that you're currently having and write it down on the lines below. Bring this with you to your next session. It will serve as your admission ticket.

_____

_____

_____

_____

_____

_____

_____

The Great Sales Debate

In a Nutshell

In this lively game, the group is divided into two teams which must debate each other to determine the best solution to a difficult sales situation.

Time

15–20 minutes.

What You'll Need

Two copies of the handout on page 137. Salespeople will need paper and pens. You will need a flip-chart and markers.

What to Do

Divide the group into two teams of equal size. Tell them that they will review a sales scenario and then hold a debate to determine what course of action should be taken by the sales representative.

Give each team a copy of the handout and assign each team a position to defend. Give them a few minutes to discuss their position and to elect a spokesperson. Then hold the debate.

As the debate takes place, you can write the "pros" of each side's position on a flip-chart or white board divided into two columns. The objective of this debate is not for one side to win but for the group to examine and discuss a diverse variety of sales issues.

Discussion Questions

Q: What did you learn from the debate?

Q: How many of you represented a position that you would not have taken if given a choice?

Q: How would a similar situation be resolved if it took place here at our organization?

If You Have More Time

Hold a second debate, this time focusing on a sales situation that the participants might face in their own jobs.

*Y*ou work at Wanamaker Widget Factory as an inside sales representative. Your company is currently facing a widget shortage and has put a temporary limit on widget sales: 2000 widgets per customer per week. One day you take a call from Alvin Zinger at South Coast Supplies. He's a longtime customer who usually orders about 4000 widgets per week. When you tell Alvin about the temporary limit on widget sales, he informs you that he'll either get 4000 widgets a week from you or he'll buy 4000 widgets from your competitor, Walla Walla Widget Factory. Argue for your team's position, regardless of what you might do if you actually faced the situation in your own job.

Team A: Your position is that the factory should make an exception for Mr. Zinger and agree to sell him 4000 widgets per week.

Team B: Your position is that Mr. Zinger should not receive more than the allotted quota of widgets.

Rules for Debate

1. All members of your team should participate in the team discussion.

2. Designate one spokesperson to argue your position.

3. You will have five minutes to discuss your position and come up with a list of reasons to support it. Then you will have two minutes to speak about why your team's course of action is the best one.

4. After each side has spoken, your team will have two minutes to come up with rebuttals to your opponents' argument. You'll then have one minute to voice your rebuttal, and the debate ends.

Problem-Busters

In a Nutshell

This game is designed to help salespeople come up with solutions to common problems in the sales environment. They benefit from the collective brain power of the group, and come away with viable answers to real-life difficulties. It's suitable for all salespeople, and it's a great way to alleviate stress and frustration.

Time

Approximately 15 minutes.

What You'll Need

An overhead transparency or a flip-chart containing the information on page 141.

What to Do

Ask the group to take a look at the overhead transparency or flip-chart and to add any general problems they commonly face as a salesperson. (At this point, the salespeople should stay away from problems that are specific to a particular customer or account.) Capture the additions on the flip-chart.

To encourage discussion, seat the salespeople in a circle. Go down the list of common problems one at a time and ask the group to brainstorm solutions or alternatives. Try to capture at least three ideas for each problem, and make sure you or someone else writes them down.

After the session, type the list of solutions under the title "Problem-Busters" and make copies for each salesperson to keep on hand.

If You're on Your Own

Develop a list of three possible solutions for each problem. You may want to brainstorm solutions with a friend or family member who is a salesperson in another industry.

Problems for Problem-Busters

- Buyer can't make a decision

- You can't get in touch with buyer

- Buyer has been with another supplier for a long time

- Buyer doesn't have the money right now

- Your company can't keep the orders filled

-

-

-

-

-

The Lost Account

In a Nutshell

In this game, participants imagine they have lost their best account and must win it back. After listing all the steps they would take, they'll check to be sure they're taking all those steps now. This game is particularly suitable for salespeople who manage large accounts.

Time

10–15 minutes.

What You'll Need

One copy of the handout on page 145 for each salesperson.

What to Do

Ask salespeople to write the name of their largest account on the handout. Now ask them to close their eyes and imagine that the phone is ringing and their contact at this account is calling to tell them that they have lost the business. The account is going to use another supplier. Have salespeople picture what would happen as a result of losing this prime account.

After 30–60 seconds, ask salespeople to open their eyes and answer the first question on the handout.

Now ask salespeople to work individually or in small groups and develop an action plan to win back the account. For example, they might meet with key contacts to review their performance, they might review the pricing structure, or they might develop other contacts within the account.

After two to three minutes, ask salespeople to review their list and place a check mark next to the actions they are already taking. If there are actions they are not already taking, ask salespeople to begin them within the next 24 hours.

Conclude the session by asking salespeople to close their eyes and visualize the successful completion of their action items and the satisfaction of key contacts at the account.

If You're on Your Own

Take a few minutes in a quiet place and imagine that you have lost your best account. Complete page 145. When you've finished, review the steps you wrote and place a check mark next to the ones you're currently taking. Make plans to complete any other steps necessary to keep this account.

My Largest Account is: _____

If I lost that account, the following would result: _____

_____

_____

Here are the steps I would take to regain my largest account:

❑   _____

_____

❑   _____

_____

❑   _____

_____

❑   _____

_____

❑   _____

_____

9

That's a Wrap!

Games for Closing and Handling Objections

Sing for Your Supper

In a Nutshell

This game provides a fun way to illustrate the importance of asking for the sale. Salespeople work alone or in pairs to write a song or jingle advertising their product and asking buyers for the sale.

Time

15 minutes.

What You'll Need

An overhead transparency or flip-chart of the information on page 151. Salespeople will need pen and paper.

What to Do

Decide whether you want the salespeople to work alone or in pairs.

Briefly discuss the importance of asking for the sale—sometimes this crucial step is forgotten or neglected by salespeople. You may want to start off by talking about the reasons why this happens, as you capture the reasons on a flip-chart.

Tell salespeople they're going to practice asking for the sale by composing a song—no musical talent required. Reveal the overhead or flip-chart and tell them to use any of the tunes to write a song presenting their product and asking for the sale.

Give salespeople seven to ten minutes to write their songs and then ask them to share their songs with the group.

Sing for Your Supper

Songs to choose from:

- **"Row, Row, Row Your Boat"**

- **"Frere Jacques"**

- **"Twinkle, Twinkle Little Star"**

- **"Rock-A-Bye Baby"**

- **"Mary Had a Little Lamb"**

- **"B-I-N-G-O"**

- **"Old MacDonald Had a Farm"**

- **"Joy to the World"**

Objection!

In a Nutshell

This is quick, lively game that gives sales-people an opportunity to practice overcoming objections.

Time

5–10 minutes.

What You'll Need

Make a copy of page 155 and cut along the lines so that you have ten pieces of paper, each with one objection on it. Put the objections into a small hat, basket, or box.

What to Do

Set up the game by defining "objection," and asking the salespeople what objections they typically receive from buyers.

Tell them that in this game, they'll practice overcoming some common objections. Select a fictional product or service to focus on during the game. One at a time, the salespeople will draw an objection out of the hat and announce it to the class; the other participants should attempt to overcome the objection. (There may be more than one response).

Before beginning the game, read the following example to the group:

Salesperson: So, Herb, when would be a good time to get started on your golf lessons?

Buyer: Well, I don't know. The price seems a little high. I'm already spending quite a bit on my golf game.

Salesperson: I look at it this way: Anytime you go out on the green, it costs money. Wouldn't you rather put some of that money toward improving your game?

Buyer: That's a good point. Sure, I'll give it a try.

If You Have More Time

Play the game again, this time with your own products or services and with the objections that your salespeople frequently encounter.

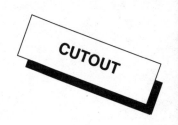

I don't like the color.

We don't need it.

It's too expensive.

I don't see any reason to switch from my present supplier.

It's not convenient.

Nobody else I know has one.

It takes too long.

We've gotten by this long without it.

Everybody would have to be taught how to use it.

I'm afraid it will be outdated too soon.

Balancing the Scales

In a Nutshell

This activity points out the importance of gathering information about the buyer's needs in order to have weight to balance against a buyer's objection. It's suitable for salespeople of all levels.

Time

10–15 minutes.

What You'll Need

A medium-sized stone to represent a buyer objection. Three smaller stones painted gold or wrapped in gold foil to represent product benefits. A cutout of a balance scale or two baskets or hats to represent the two sides of a balance scale.

What to Do

Review the concept of uncovering buyer's needs and presenting benefits to match those needs. Discuss how those previously accepted benefits can be used like pieces of gold to outweigh customer objections that come up later in the sales call.

Ask salespeople to call out common objections they face in their sales calls. List them on a flip-chart or white board and select two, four, or six depending on the time available for the game.

Divide the group into two teams. Flip a coin or use another method to determine which team will go first. Take the first objection and put the stone representing the objection onto the left side of the "scale." Tell the first team that they will have 30 seconds to add three pieces of gold to the right side of the scale in order to balance the scales. Each gold piece will represent one benefit. Say, for example, that the stone represents the objection "It doesn't come in red." In that case, the three pieces of gold might represent the following benefits:

1. It is less expensive.
2. It can be personalized to reinforce the company slogan.
3. It made of higher quality materials and won't have to be replaced as often.

Assign one point for every piece of gold that is added to the right side and one extra point if the team adds three pieces of gold to the scale.

Select another objection and let the second team balance the scales. Continue until you've balanced the scales for all objections. Tally the score and award a small prize to the winning team.

If You Have More Time

Ask salespeople to develop a list of questions they might use to uncover the benefits that can overcome common objections.

If You're on Your Own

Make a list of the objections you most frequently encounter. Work by yourself or with a friend or co-worker to develop a list of possible benefits that you might use to outweigh each objection.

It Costs How Much?

In a Nutshell

In this game, salespeople practice overcoming price objections for everyday
products. It is suitable for all levels of salespeople.

Time

15–20 minutes.

What You'll Need

One copy of page 163 for every eight participants. A hat,
box, or basket.

What to Do

Discuss that price objections can often be overcome by
reminding the buyer of product benefits he or she found
valuable. Tell salespeople that they are going to work in
pairs to practice overcoming price objections.

Cut the copies of page 163 into individual scenarios
and place them in a hat, box, or basket. Arrange sales people into pairs and have each pair draw one scenario. The
pairs are to work together to develop a statement that they
hope will overcome a price objection. They should also
develop a question to confirm that they have successfully
overcome the objection.

Read the following example to the group:

If a buyer accepted benefits related to memory, speed, and size of a notebook computer and objected to the price, the salesperson might say, "The price might seem to be a little higher, but let's look at the total package. This computer has twice as much memory. It's always less expensive to purchase memory with your computer, rather than to add it later, because you avoid the labor costs. The faster processing speed means you'll have information on your screen in seconds and avoid the frustration of sitting there waiting for programs and data to load. You also said you travel a lot and the lighter weight and smaller size of this notebook was attractive. All told, don't you feel that those advantages outweigh the slightly higher price?"

Give salespeople three or four minutes to develop their statements, then have each group share their scenario and their statement out loud.

If You Have More Time

Have salespeople play the game again, this time with product scenarios from your own company that you have prepared in advance.

If You're on Your Own

Write a statement and a confirming question to overcome each price objection on page 163.

Overcoming Price Objections

Scenario One

You're a sales representative for Six Seas Travel. You're talking with Mr. and Mrs. Alfonse about your upcoming cruise. The Alfonses have accepted benefits related to the 24-hour buffet, the onboard observatory, and the morning and evening tango lessons. When you present the price, Mrs. Alfonse shrieks, "It costs how much?"

Scenario Two

You're a sales representative for Sun-Daze showing a patio set to Ella Ng. She's accepted benefits related to the unique green and purple striped umbrella, the matching polka-dot chairs (she thinks she'll be the talk of the neighborhood), and the fact that the set has a six-year warranty against sun fading. When you present the price she screams, "It costs how much?"

Scenario Three

Jimmy Rae Jones wants to get in shape but keeps putting off exercising. He's looking at your new sports watch and has accepted benefits related to the pulse indicator, the built-in odometer, and the fact that the alarm will not turn off until he has walked one mile. When you present the price, Jimmy Rae shrieks, "It costs how much?"

Scenario Four

You work for Trip the Light Fantastic dance studio. Rae Jones is considering dance lessons and has accepted benefits related to the convenient location of the studio, the number of eligible bachelors at each class, and the fact that cake and punch are served during the break. When you present the price of the class, she faints and, upon revival, asks, "It costs how much?"

10

That's Not All!

Games for Cross-Selling and Up-Selling

It's Not Just a Fruit

In a Nutshell

In this game, participants learn to cross-sell or substitute-sell by outlining the features and benefits of common "products" such as a banana. The game helps salespeople to quickly and creatively recognize a product's benefits.

Time

10 minutes.

What You'll Need

An overhead transparency or flip-chart with the information on page 170. Blank flip-chart paper and marker pens.

What to Do

Using the overhead transparency, discuss the concepts of features and benefits. Remind salespeople that customers buy benefits, not features, and that pointing out benefits is particularly important when trying to cross-sell or substitute-sell.

Put salespeople into groups of three to five. Explain that their job is to work together to develop a list of features and benefits for some common "products."

Assign one product from the following list to each group.

- A banana
- A safety pin
- A lollipop
- A cat
- A rose
- A chocolate-chip cookie

Hand out a piece of blank flip-chart paper and a pen to each group. Ask participants to list the features of their product and then to list the corresponding benefits. One way to find benefits is to ask, "So what?" For example: "Our sunscreen has an SPF of 15." "So what?" "So you can stay in the sun longer without burning."

After four or five minutes, ask each group to present the features and benefits of their product. Ask "So what?" after each feature until the group agrees that a compelling benefit has been presented.

If You Have More Time

Have each group develop a feature and benefit chart for one of their company's products. After presentations have been made, prepare an attractive copy of the feature and benefit information and distribute it for use on the job.

If You're on Your Own

Review the definitions of features and benefits on page 170 and then develop a list of features and benefits for each of the products listed on page 168. Then develop a list of features and benefits for your own products or services.

Features and Benefits

A **feature** is a distinct part or quality of a product or service.

"Our sun block has an SPF of 15."

A **benefit** is the value of the feature to the customer.

"This means you can sit out in the sun longer without burning."

Product Partners

In a Nutshell

Salespeople are assigned products to represent, and they mingle with one another to establish as many "partnerships" as they can based on a commonality between their two products. This game reinforces creative thinking and the ability to establish relationships between diverse objects. It's ideal for salespeople who need to cross-sell.

Time

10–15 minutes.

What You'll Need

One copy of the product list on page 174. A hat, bag, or basket. Salespeople will also need paper and pens and may want a clipboard or other hard surface for writing.

What to Do

Cut the copy of the product list from page 174 into pieces so that you have 16 slips of paper, each with the name of one product. Put these in the "hat."

Tell salespeople that they'll select a product to represent and then go around the room to talk to other salespeople to try to establish partnerships based on a commonality between their products. The objective is to create as many partnerships as they can in the allotted time.

For example, someone who sells oranges might be able to create a partnership with someone who sells apples because they both sell fruit. The same person could create a partnership with someone who sells balls because their respective products are both round.

Salespeople should work with one another to establish relationships between their products, but they should not spend more than one or two minutes with each potential partner. None of the salespeople will be able to establish partnerships with everyone they talk to. Each time they establish a partnership, they should record their partner and the product relationship on a piece of paper.

Once you've explained the game, ask salespeople to draw a product from the "hat" and begin the game. After about ten minutes, stop the game and ask for volunteers to share their results.

Trainer Note: Countless combinations are possible. Following are just a few:

1. Things people use at work (telephone, books, paper, computer, cardboard boxes, eyeglasses)

2. Things people like to receive as gifts (flowers, clothing, chocolates, music tapes, and CDs)

3. Things people put on their coffee table at home (flowers, books, chocolates)

4. Things people use to communicate (telephones, computers, pens, paper, musical instruments)

5. Things almost everyone owns (telephone, cars, books, shoes, televisions)

6. Things you pay tax on (everything)

7. Things that die (flowers, cars)

If You Have More Time

Ask salespeople to work in small groups to develop "product partners" for their products and services.

If You're on Your Own

This is less of a game if you're working alone, but it's still a great exercise for creative thinking. Following the examples shown above, create as many partnerships as you can among the products on page 174.

Product List

You sell books.	You sell paper.
You sell telephones.	You sell shoes.
You sell computer equipment.	You sell musical instruments.
You sell pens and pencils.	You sell cardboard boxes.
You sell flowers.	You sell eyeglasses.
You sell chocolates.	You sell furniture.
You sell clothing.	You sell cars.
You sell sporting goods.	You sell televisions.

And by the Way . . .

In a Nutshell

Salespeople learn to identify opportunities for up-selling, and they practice up-selling. This game is suitable for those salespeople who have the opportunity to increase order value, particularly those who are new to sales.

Time

5–10 minutes.

What You'll Need

One copy of the handout on page 177 for each salesperson. One copy of page 178 for every four salespeople. A hat, box, or basket.

What to Do

Distribute and review the handout on page 177. Tell salespeople that they'll work in pairs to practice up-selling.

Cut the copies of page 178 into individual scenarios and place them in a hat, box, or basket. Arrange salespeople into pairs and ask each pair to draw one scenario. The pairs are to work together to develop an up-selling statement. For example, assume the scenario drawn says, "The customer orders a a gross of pencils. See if the customer is interested in saving five cents per pencil by ordering two gross." In this case, the statement might be, "That was 144 pencils at sixty-five cents each. You know, Elliott, I can lower your price by five cents per pencil if you order two gross. Would that work for you?"

Give the pairs two to three minutes to develop their statement, then ask them to share their statement with the group.

If You Have More Time

Talk about up-selling opportunities in the salespeople's real-time environment, and play the game again using actual product scenarios.

If You're on Your Own

Review page 177 and then develop up-selling statements for each scenario on page 178. Then try your hand at writing up-selling statements for some of your real-life sales situations.

Up-Selling

When you up-sell, you increase the value of an order by asking the customer to commit to a higher quantity. This is typically done when customers can obtain a price break or another perk if they purchase at a higher quantity. When up-selling, always point out a benefit to the customer (we've underlined the benefit to show you what we mean). Up-selling sounds like this:

Mr. Smith, I can <u>drop that price for you by $2.48</u> on each unit if you can increase your order by two cases. Does that make sense for you?

John, we're having a special offer this week that will help you <u>lower your cost</u>. I can offer you 25% off if you order at least 100. Would you like to do that?

I saw you looking at that great travel mug. You know, if you purchase $45 worth of merchandise today, you can get one of those mugs <u>free</u>! Can I show you some of our line?

The steps for up-selling are as follows:

1. Explain how the customer can save money by increasing the order. Be sure to point out a benefit to the customer.

2. Ask the customer to commit to a larger order.

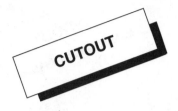

Up-Selling

Scenario One

You work for the local repertory theater. One customer bought advance tickets for three of the seven plays showing at your theater this season.
The tickets are $35.00 each. See if he would be interested in buying season tickets for a total of $200.00 per seat.

Scenario Two

You work in a clothing shop. A customer is just about to purchase two pairs of socks for $4.99 a pair. The store currently has a special of five pairs for $19.99. See if the customer would be interested in increasing the number of pairs in order to save money.

Scenario Three

You work in a computer store and you've been answering questions for Jim about your lowest-priced computer. It seems as if price is very important to Jim, but you know that a computer that costs $150 more also includes three software packages that might be useful. This upgrade would save Jim $650 over the price of the lower-priced computer plus the software. See if Jim is interested in this upgrade.

Scenario Four

You sell restaurant supplies. A regular customer wants to order one case each of 10-ounce and 12-ounce paper cups. You currently have a special running: If a customer orders four cases of any cups, they can get a fifth case free.

Would You Like Fries with Your Burger?

In a Nutshell

Salespeople learn when and how to cross-sell when talking with customers. This game is ideal for salespeople who have the opportunity to increase order value by using this technique.

Time

5–10 minutes.

What You'll Need

One copy of the handout on page 181 for each participant. One copy of page 182 for every eight salespeople. A hat, box, or basket.

What to Do

Distribute and review the handout on page 181. Tell salespeople that they are going to work in pairs to practice cross-selling.

Cut the copies of page 182 into individual scenarios and place them in a hat, box, or basket. Arrange salespeople into pairs and have each pair draw one scenario.

The pairs are to work together to develop a cross-selling statement. For example, assume the scenario said, "The customer orders a top hat. See if the customer is also interested in gloves or a cane." In this case, the statement might be, "By the way, Mr. Astaire, we also have some high-quality gloves and a very handsome cane that would look smashing with your top hat. Would you like me to tell you more about them?"

Give the pairs two to three minutes to develop their statement; then have them share their statement out loud.

If You Have More Time

Have salespeople play the game again, this time with product scenarios from your own company that you have prepared in advance.

If You're on Your Own

Review page 181, then develop a cross-selling statement for each scenario on page 182. When you've finished, consider which of your own products are suitable for cross-selling, then develop some statements to help you cross-sell on your next sales call.

Cross-Selling

When you cross-sell, you increase the value of an order by selling the customer complementary products. When cross-selling, you should always point out a benefit to the customer. We've underlined the benefit in the examples below to show you what we mean. Cross-selling sounds like this:

You know, Nancy, many of our customers who order our "Poster Maker" software also like to get the $12.95 deluxe clip-art package. It's a <u>great value</u>, it's very <u>easy to use</u>, and it gives you 250 images that make your posters really <u>attractive</u>. Would you like me to send the clip-art to you along with "Poster Maker?"

To confirm, I'll send you 144 ninety-minute XR-90 cassette tapes. By the way, we're having a special on our sixty-minute XZ-60 tapes and you can <u>save 15%</u>. Do you use sixty-minute tapes?

That shirt looks fantastic on you, Mr. Zoot. Let me show you a tie that will look great with it. The nice thing about this tie is that it not only goes with this shirt, but you can also wear it with a blue or white shirt. It's very <u>versatile</u> and it's a <u>good quality</u> tie at a very <u>affordable price</u>. Would you like to add it to your wardrobe?

The steps for cross-selling are as follows:

1. Make a statement to bridge from the product the customer has ordered to the product you want to cross-sell.

2. Describe the product you want to cross-sell and point out its benefits.

3. Ask the customer to buy it.

Cross-Selling

Scenario One

Jermaine Montez bought two tickets for a 15-day cruise to the Virgin Islands. You know he and his wife like to scuba dive. See if they'd like to have a guided dive through the underwater park off St. John, some of the most beautiful underwater scenery available in the Caribbean. It's four hours, includes a basket lunch, and costs $150 per person.

Scenario Two

Ms. Pottsbough has just ordered a very expensive desk pad from your catalog of exclusive desk accessories. See if she is interested in the matching pen set and letter tray. The entire set just won the coveted Milano award for office furnishings, and there are only 250 sets available. The pen set and letter tray retail for $685.

Scenario Three

Jimmy Rae Jones has just signed up for your weekly Mow-and-Trim lawn-care service. You know that lawns look better and are less expensive to maintain over time if your patented Weed-and-Feed solution is applied quarterly. This additional service adds $25 to the bill each month, but it can save money and time in weeding and re-seeding.

Scenario Four

Mossie Smart has been shopping in your store for drapery fabric. It's clear that she is uncertain about how to make the drapes herself. You also offer sewing services, and although it would cost Mossie $400 to have the drapes made, the fabric is $700 and could easily be ruined by a cutting or sewing error.

Cheaper by the Dozen

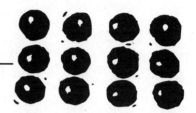

In a Nutshell

Salespeople work together to identify advantages to customers of buying larger quantities of selected products. This game is ideal for new or relatively inexperienced salespeople—it helps them to understand the basic sales principle of up-selling.

Time

10–15 minutes.

What You'll Need

An overhead transparency or flip-chart of the information on page 185. Salespeople will need paper and pen.

What to Do

Set up the game by asking the group what products they buy in large quantities and why.

Divide the salespeople into teams of two or three, and reveal the overhead or flip-chart. Ask them to come up with advantages to customers of buying larger quantities of the products. Encourage them to come up with multiple advantages for each product.

Let salespeople know that the advantages don't have to be only for individual buyers. They should consider the fact that the buyer might be a company or other organization.

After seven to ten minutes, go down the list of products and ask each group what advantages they identified. Wrap up the game by discussing the advantages to customers of buying large quantities of the products represented by the salespeople.

If You're on Your Own

Review the list of products on pave 185. For each item, try to identify at least three advantages of buying large quantities.

Cheaper by the Dozen

- **Paper towels**

- **Printer cartridges**

- **Pens**

- **Bottled water**

- **Movie tickets**

- **Socks**

- **Computers**

II

Spelling Counts

Activities for Communications Excellence behind the Scenes

Wares Whaldo?

In a Nutshell

Participants are given a sales letter filled with common grammatical errors and must identify and replace as many as they can.

Time

10 minutes.

What You'll Need

An overhead transparency or flip-chart of the information on page 191. One copy of the letter on page 192 for each participant.

What to Do

Begin the activity by holding a brief discussion about the importance of good written communication between salespeople and their buyers. Why does it matter? What causes poor letter-writing? What are the essential elements of good written communication?

Hand out the letter and tell salespeople to work alone or in pairs to identify and correct the errors. Tell them to follow the guidelines on the flip-chart. Note: If you are doing this activity with a particularly competitive or perfectionistic group, you may need to coach them as to how far to go with their corrections. Let them know that the content of the letter is fine, but that there are several obvious, common errors in the writing.

Once they've finished the activity, ask the salespeople what errors they found and how they corrected them. Use the letter on page 193 as the answer key.

If You're on Your Own

Read the instructions on page 191. Review the letter on page 192 and make the appropriate corrections. When you've finished, check your answers on page 193.

Instructions

Do:

- Correct spelling
- Correct punctuation
- Correct grammatical mistakes

Don't:

Rewrite the letter

COPIERS R US

463 Toner Lane
Oakville, CA 92665 • 800-555-3346

March 1, 1999

Ms. Susan Lewis,
Artwald Enterprises
31 Roughy Road
Lakeville, CA 92199

Dear Susan:

Thank you for your time on the phone last Thursday: I enjoyed our conversation and I look forward too meeting you in person at 9:00 a.m. on the morning of March 14.

It sounds to me like the ProGen 2700 is a perfect fit for your photocopier needs. its designed for high-volume use and has a great maintenance track record. Best of all, the price of the the copier is within your budget!

I'm enclosing some brochures on the ProGen 2700 and it's ancillary products. Feel free to call me anytime at 619/555-9047 if you any questions.

Sincereley,

Brad

Brad Forseth
Sales Associate

COPIERS R US

463 Toner Lane
Oakville, CA 92665 • 800-555-3346

March 1, 1999

Remove comma

Ms. Susan Lewis,
Artwald Enterprises
31 Roughy Road
Lakeville, CA 92199

Should be a period

Dear Susan:

Thank you for your time on the phone last Thursday: I enjoyed our conversation and I look forward too meeting you in person at 9:00 a.m. on the morning of March 14.

to

Redundant. A.M. means morning

It sounds to me like the ProGen 2700 is a perfect fit for your photocopier needs. its designed for high-volume use and has a great maintenance track record. Best of all, the price of the the copier is within your budget!

It's

"the" appears twice

< Close up this space by one line

Its

I'm enclosing some brochures on the ProGen 2700 and it's ancillary products. Feel free to call me anytime at 619-555-9047 if you any questions.

have

Sincereley, ◄——— *Sincerely*

Brad

Brad Forseth
Sales Associate

Short, Sweet, and to the Point

In a Nutshell

Salespeople work together to rewrite abstruse statement to more concisely convey sales benefits. This activity is suitable for salespeople who sell complex products and who need to convey product benefits concisely to buyers. It's also ideal for new salespeople who need to learn to be concise.

Time

10–15 minutes.

What You'll Need

One copy of the handout on page 197 for each salesperson. Salespeople will each need a pen.

What to Do

Divide the salespeople into teams of two or three. Review the concept of features and benefits and remind them that buyers need to hear benefits that are strong, clear, and concise.

Distribute one handout to each salesperson. Ask them to work in their teams to rewrite each of the two statements into a strong, clear, and concise benefit statement.

While the teams are rewriting their statements, take a look at the possible answers on page 198. Their responses should be similar to these.

After about five minutes, ask each team to present its first revised statement. Have the group vote on the most clear and concise statement. Present the winning team with a small reward or acknowledgment

Give teams another minute to review the second statement and to make any changes they feel would tighten it up. Then ask each team to present its second revised statement. Once again, take a vote and present the winning team with a small reward or acknowledgment.

If You're on Your Own

Rewrite the statements on page 197 so that they become strong, clear, and concise statements of benefits.

1. Well, Mr. Barrows, if you decide to go with our Be Prepared flashlights, it seems like it might cost less than what you're paying now—and they're really reliable. I think you said you now get about ten gross every quarter and pay about $6.50 each. If you got ours, you could save about $1.00 on each one. (Note: There are 144 in a gross).

_____

_____

_____

_____

_____

2. Well, if you have to call up your current courier service and then wait until they get everything in your neighborhood consolidated before they can pick your package up, I bet that gets frustrating some times. As you know, we can pick things up anytime you call us. As a matter of fact, we guarantee we'll show up within two hours after you call. Since you work on your own, and you're sometimes out of the office, you said it gets tricky. When that happens, you can drop off your package at our office down the street if that's easier for you. Whatever makes you happiest!

_____

_____

_____

_____

_____

Possible answers:

1. Mr. Barrows, by switching to the reliable Be Prepared flashlight, you can save close to $6,000 per year.

2. You're a busy professional, and we respect your time by offering you two convenient options. We'll either pick up your package within two hours of your call, or you can drop it off at our office. It's just two doors down.

Common Questions

In a Nutshell

Salespeople work in groups to answer basic questions—who, what, where, when, why, and how—about their products. This game is ideal for educating new salespeople and for increasing salespeople's knowledge about new products so that they can write or speak clearly and concisely about their product or service.

Time

5–15 minutes, depending on the number of rounds you play.

What You'll Need

Several pieces of flip-chart paper and markers. An overhead transparency or flip-chart containing the information on page 201.

What to Do

Identify one or more products that will be described during the game. Plan to complete one round of the game for each distinct product.

Divide the group into six pairs or teams, and give each a piece of flip-chart paper and a marker. Show the overhead or flip-chart of the information on page 201, and assign each team one of the questions. Note: If the group has fewer than twelve salespeople, make fewer teams and assign each team more than one question.

Tell the group that you'll announce a product and their job is to answer the assigned question as completely as possible. Announce the product and give them an adequate amount of time to come up with their answers (time will vary according to the complexity of the product and the knowledge of the salespeople). Encourage them to think "outside the box" in brainstorming their answers.

After a few minutes, ask each team to report its answers to the group.

For each new round, give salespeople a new sheet of flip-chart paper and assign each team a different question.

If You're on Your Own

Consider each of your major products or services and answer the questions on page 201. Develop clear and succinct answers that you can use in written and spoken communication.

Common Questions

- Who is it for?

- What does it do?

- Where is it used?

- When is it used?

- Why is it used?

- How is it used?

12

Come on In

Games to Enhance Retail Sales

If I Could Do Anything

In a Nutshell

Pairs compete in a mock contest to come up
with ideas for promoting their products and
making sales. This game aims to get salespeople thinking creatively about the many ways to attract
customers and to serve their needs. The contest works best
with five to eight pairs and is suitable for salespeople at all
levels.

Time

15–20 minutes.

What You'll Need

Make one copy of the fictional businesses on pages 207 and
208. Cut the sheets so that you have several slips of paper,
each with one business on it. You'll also need a hat, bowl,
or basket in which to put the slips of paper so that the participants can randomly draw them.

What to Do

Tell the group that they'll be participating in a Creative
Sales Contest sponsored by the local community business
association. They'll be given a fictional business to represent
and work in pairs to come up with an idea for the contest.

The purpose of the contest is to come up with an idea that will both promote the business and offer something special to customers. Encourage participants to be as creative as possible in coming up with their ideas. There are no budgetary restrictions, but entries must be "reasonable." The ideas should relate to the business; for example, a grocery store couldn't offer free puppies.

Share the following sample entry with the participants to give them an idea of how the game works:

Name of company: Millennium Bank
Line of business: Bank
Idea: We're going to give free checking for life to every 2000th person who signs up for a Millennium checking or savings account.

Assign pairs and ask one representative from each pair to pick a slip of paper from the "hat." Give participants about ten minutes to come up with their ideas, and then go around the room and have each pair announce their business and their idea. Then take a vote to see who wins the contest.

If You Have More Time

After the activity, you can ask pairs to come up with creative ideas for promoting their own product or service to customers.

Name of company: **The Game of Life**

Line of business: **Sporting goods manufacturer**

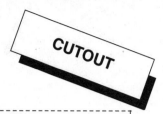

Idea: _____

_____

_____

Name of company: **Quo Vadis?**

Line of business: **Shuttle service**

Idea: _____

_____

_____

Name of company: **Netware**

Line of business: **Internet service provider**

Idea: _____

_____

_____

Name of company: **Beauty and the Beast**

Line of business: **Salon and barber shop supplies**

Idea: _____

_____

_____

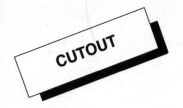

Name of company: **Call on Me**

Line of business: **Cellular phone service**

Idea: _____

_____

_____

Name of company: **Page One Press**

Line of business: **Book distributor**

Idea: _____

_____

_____

Name of company: **Ritzy Retreads**

Line of business: **Used luxury cars**

Idea: _____

_____

_____

Name of company: **The City Zoo**

Line of business: **One of the country's largest zoos**

Idea: _____

_____

_____

Come on In!

In a Nutshell

This is a quick, fun game you can play anytime to energize retail salespeople and help them inject creativity and enthusiasm into their job. The objective of this game is to help retail salespeople find new ways to greet and approach customers.

Time

2–5 minutes.

What You'll Need

A small, soft ball or similar object.

What to Do

Ask the participants to stand in a circle a few feet apart, and tell them that they're going to practice coming up with alternatives to the standard phrase, "May I help you?" When someone catches the ball, they must respond with a statement that can be used to greet or approach customers.

Begin the game by tossing the ball to someone, and continue until everyone has had at least one chance to respond.

Tip! This game can be used to give salespeople practice in other aspects of their job as well: thanking customers, saying goodbye, cross-selling, up-selling, etc.

If You're on Your Own

Develop a few alternatives to the standard phrase, "May I help you?" To help you think of alternatives, brainstorm with a friend or another salesperson.

Service Spoken Here

In a Nutshell

In this activity, salespeople brainstorm creative ideas for serving their customers. This activity is best for salespeople who have a clear understanding of customer service.

Time

10–15 minutes.

What You'll Need

A flip-chart or white board and marker pen. Blank paper.

What to Do

Put participants in groups of three or four. Tell them to imagine that they made the rules regarding what could be done for their customers. Ask them what measures—small or large—they might take to serve their customers better.

Tell them to be specific; for example, rather than say, "I'd have cleaner dressing rooms," they should say, "I'd set up a rotating schedule so one of us cleared the dressing room of clothes every 30 minutes."

Give each group a blank sheet of paper to record their thoughts.

After five minutes, ask each group to report on the results of their brainstorming. List answers on a flip-chart or white board.

Determine which ideas can be implemented right away, and ask participants to put them into practice. For those ideas that require further research and/or management's approval, make a list to review with management. Be sure to let participants know the outcome.

If You're on Your Own

Develop a list of measures—small or large—that you might take to provide better service for your customers. Put into practice those that you can implement on your own right away. Discuss the rest with your manager.

Make It Personal

In a Nutshell

This game helps salespeople to realize that there are literally hundreds of ways they can impress and encourage potential buyers. Each salesperson uses the letters of his or her name to come up with an action or behavior that helps them in sales situations. It's a fun activity to use as an energizing "filler" or as a warm-up to a more intensive sales training session.

Time

10 minutes.

What You'll Need

Each salesperson will need a piece of paper and a pen. You'll need a flip-chart or white board and markers.

What to Do

Tell each salesperson to write his or her name vertically along the center of a sheet of paper. Demonstrate by writing the following on a flip-chart or white board:

M
A
R
Y

Now their task is to use each letter of their name to come up with an action that they can take to impress or encourage potential buyers. Each letter of their name must begin a word in the action phrase, but it doesn't necessarily have to be the first word of the phrase. Actions can be phrased either positively (Do . . .) or negatively (Don't . . .). For example:

Look **M**arvelous.
    Ask for the sale
    Respect their needs.
Don't say **Y**es unless I'm sure I can follow through.

Encourage the group to have fun with this activity and to be as creative as possible. Almost anything goes!

After seven or eight minutes, ask for some volunteers to share what they came up with. Point out that there are hundreds, even thousands of ways to get the sale.

Tip! If the participants like what they come up with, they can post it at their workstation.

If You're on Your Own

Follow the steps outlined above, and repeat the activity two or three times so that you'll see a variety of actions.